MONOLOGUES

—— THEY'LL ——

REMEMBER
YOU BY

MONOLOGUES

— THEY'LL —

REMEMBER
YOU BY

80 Unique and Compelling
Monologues That Leave
a Lasting Impression

ANDREW BISS

ENTR'ACTE
EDITIONS

2017

Original cover image © Lofilolo
Cover design by Ernest Waggenheim

First Edition

Copyright © 2017 Andrew Biss

All rights reserved.

ISBN: 1974174859
ISBN-13: 978-1974174850

ENTR'ACTE
EDITIONS

"The first step to a better audition is to give up character and use yourself."

~ Michael Shurtleff

CONTENTS

COMEDIC MONOLOGUES

DRAMATIC MONOLOGUES

SERIOCOMIC MONOLOGUES

INTRODUCTION

What is a perfect monologue? In truth, there is no one-size-fits-all template for a performance piece, since all actors are different and every audition will come with its own unique set of requirements. However, not all monologues are created equal, and there are plenty of imperfect examples available that are more likely to hobble than help your chances of winning that coveted role or competition.

Ideally, an audition monologue should resemble a miniature one-person play; a self-contained story that has its own beginning, middle and end (or punch line), no matter how brief or abstract it may be. It should require little or no explanation to give it context and meaning because the one commodity that most casting directors have in very short supply is time. And above all else, it should make an impact.

As an actor or drama student, that brief moment in the spotlight you're given to show what you're capable of can seem mercilessly fleeting – because it is. But that is precisely the reason you need to be as wise and judicious as possible in selecting a monologue that's going to demonstrate your skill set in the best possible light in such a short space of time. Monologues that they've heard trotted out a million times before or that lean toward the timid or ponderous are going to have them looking at their watches before you've barely made it out of the gate. To co-opt one of my favorite Noël Coward quotes: "Consider casting directors. Never fear them nor despise them. Coax them, charm them, interest them, stimulate them, shock them now and then if you must, make them laugh, make them cry, but above all never, never, never bore the living hell out of them."

Consequently, in compiling this book I've attempted to create a valuable resource for both professional and student actors that provides opportunities to make a lasting impression on potentially jaded ears. As a former actor, when I first began writing plays I vowed I would never write a line of dialogue I wouldn't be happy to perform myself. Likewise, in assembling this collection I've sought to include only those monologues that meet the aforementioned criteria and that my former self would have felt proud and confident stepping into the spotlight with.

So, commit, be brave, be bold, and most of all...break that leg!

A FEW THINGS TO CONSIDER

While you might feel compelled to dive straight in and begin reading through all of the various monologues contained herein, there are one or two things you may wish to consider before deciding whether or not a particular monologue is right for you.

AGE RANGES

While I've endeavored to give each monologue as broad an age range as seems realistically feasible, that shouldn't deter you from thinking beyond my guidelines and putting a different spin on them if you think you can pull it off. Unless the monologue contains information that clearly suggests the character must be of a certain age, there is absolutely no reason why you shouldn't look beyond the range I've suggested.

As an example, I recently had a production of my short play *The Skewed Picture* staged at a theatre in Spokane, Washington. As written, the play has a cast of one woman and one man who portray a middle-aged married couple. During the casting process, the director contacted me and asked if I would be willing to allow him to cast two thirty-something women – which, in retrospect, could equally have been two twenty-something women – as the married couple, as the two actors from the auditions that had the best chemistry were both younger women. Surprised but delighted by the idea, I trusted his judgment, changed "Bob" to "Barb" and wished them luck. As it turned out, the concept worked perfectly, the actors did a truly outstanding job, and I couldn't have been more pleased with the production.

So, even though I frequently attempt think outside the box in my writing, it might be worth your while to consider thinking outside of mine.

You might also notice on occasion that the age range of the same character may differ from one monologue to another. This is because one of them may contain some age-defining information, but another may not, rendering the character's age as originally written as irrelevant for our purposes. Remember, you're not performing the entire play, just a few words from one character, so unless warranted by what's in the text, the same rules needn't apply.

GENDER

The previous example should also serve to illustrate the importance of sometimes looking beyond the gender of a character as written. As with age ranges, unless there is something contained within the text itself that necessitates the character being a certain gender, look beyond the given information. Feel free to change the name of a character accordingly, or ask me for a suggestion if you like. The important thing is for you to find the right monologues to best display your talent, and if that necessitates a little tweaking in the process, then so be it.

You'll notice, too, that a number of these monologues have already been given a *cross-castable* notation. But again, if you come across ones that haven't and you feel a strong connection to the character, go ahead and adapt the gender to fit your own wherever practicable.

ACCENTS

You will occasionally come across a monologue that, as written, may have a specific accent. I say *may* because, of course, it will depend upon your own regional origins or nationality as to whether it does or doesn't. I also say *may have* rather than *requires* an accent, as more often than not you'll be able to perform the monologue in your native accent – should you wish to do so – with just the tiniest amount of tinkering. In almost all cases, changing *I ain't* to *I'm not* or *I haven't*, or *nothin'* to *nothing*, for instance, can allow you to adapt the text to suit your natural pronunciation without diluting the impact or the emotional tone of the piece.

A perfect example here would be an early production of my one-act play *Cuthbert's Last Stand* that was staged at the American Globe Theatre in New York some years ago. The play is centered on an upper middle class family in suburban England. However, in rehearsal the cast were struggling with their English accents, so rather than have the distraction of dodgy diction, the decision was made to switch the setting to the American South, with the requisite Southern American accents. It was something I would never have considered under normal circumstances, but if that was what it took to rescue the production then I just had to go along with it and hope for the best. Yet, despite my reservations and to my great relief, it worked like a charm.

That experience, along with the previously mentioned one in

Spokane – and others in between – served as valuable lessons in not getting too hamstrung by my own preconceptions of what I'd originally put down on paper.

LENGTH

You'll find that most of these monologues have a running time of approximately 2 minutes or less, that being the average length of an audition time slot. Some are a little longer, as are some audition time slots. But if you connect with a monologue that runs longer than your allotted time, don't be coy about trimming it down to fit your needs, as long as what you remove doesn't adversely affect the arc of the story. The last thing you want to do is rush your performance.

MATURE LANGUAGE

By which, of course, I refer not to some sort of highly evolved speech pattern, but to profanity. To be clear, instances of profanity in this collection are few and far between. As a playwright, I've never used it gratuitously in my work, but at the same time I've never shied away from including it whenever it seemed appropriate to the character or the situation. To do otherwise strikes me as dishonest writing. That said, however, some may be uncomfortable speaking it, and indeed there is the very real risk of offending the sensibilities of those you're performing in front of. Therefore, I would suggest one of the following:

    a)   Remove the word(s) from the monologue entirely.

b) Replace the word(s) with something more palatable. If choosing this option, though, I would recommend paying careful attention to finding a replacement word(s) that conveys the same degree of intensity as the original. For instance, replacing the *f* word with *damn* or *goddamn* (if you're okay with a little blasphemy) works, as in: "I'll rip your goddamn head off!" Whereas, replacing it with something like *cotton-picking* doesn't, as in: "I'll rip your cotton-picking head off!" You get the idea.

Again, there aren't many instances of profanity in this collection, and some have already been modified from their original form for this publication. But should you find one in a monologue that you feel particularly drawn to, simply use your own judgment in deciding what to do with it.

FINAL THOUGHTS

Although these monologues have been separated into comedic, dramatic and seriocomic, many of them will have a little drama mixed in with the comedy and vice versa. The benefit of this, of course, is that not only does it allow you to show a little more range and nuance, but I've always found the best comedy to be tinged with a hint of darkness, and all good drama to resonate stronger with the infusion of a little humor, be it black, sardonic or otherwise.

The vast majority of the monologues here have been taken directly from the source play in their complete and original form. A small number of them, however, have been amalgamated from stretches of dialogue where the responses from the other character in the scene have been removed, with occasional modifications made to ensure flow and clarity.

During my days as an actor, I would often be frustrated by the dearth of interesting monologues that hadn't already been flogged to death at countless audition calls. So I took to creating my own. I discovered that although a character's best dialogue often wasn't embedded in a monologue, I could – with a few adjustments and a little poetic license – fashion a monologue of my liking through my own innovation.

And that's really what I'm trying to impress upon you here. The success of your performance is paramount, so don't be afraid to take any of the monologues in this book and make them work for you, even if at first glance they may not appear to. If it's for a man and you're a woman, or vice versa, perhaps a name change and the omission of a word or line or two will make it work. If you like a monologue but the character has an accent you're not comfortable with, do it in your own, adapting words wherever necessary. If a character's older and you're younger, or vice versa, do it anyway, removing any age-related information if it'll still work without it.

Plays are meant to be performed as written, but monologues aren't plays; they're short presentation pieces intended to help you win that role or competition. Audition panels and casting directors aren't going to give you any extra points for sticking faithfully to the source material. The only thing they care about is seeing you deliver a knockout performance of whatever it is you've chosen to present them with.

Hopefully you'll find plenty of examples here that will fit your needs perfectly just as they are. But if there are others that really speak to you but don't match your age range, gender or native accent, by all means go ahead and tinker with them.

I really won't mind, I promise. And let's face it…I'll never know.

COMEDIC MONOLOGUES

Female

CAROLINE

Age range: Late teens – 30s

From the play *Indigenous Peoples*, included in the collection *A Ballyhoo in Blighty*.

Caroline, a rather flighty, superficial young woman, is trying to adjust to the rigors of life in the great outdoors after agreeing to a weekend camping trip with her boyfriend, Roger. Upon realizing that she has no cell phone signal, however, panic sets in at the thought of not being able to reach her psychoanalyst, prompting Roger to casually inquire as to why she has one in the first place.

Why do I have a psychoanalyst? Well, actually, it was a gift if you must know, from Daddy for my fourteenth birthday – which was really quite thoughtful of him, considering he wasn't a thoughtful man by nature. But you see, Mummy had just recently run off and abandoned us, so he thought it might be quite nice to get me something practical, that I could use, rather than something frivolous like a new dress, say, or a doll. *(Beat.)* Mummy adapted very well to her new life, from all accounts. She'd absconded with a rather bulbous, but frighteningly wealthy gentleman from the Federated States of Micronesia. Their president, apparently…or tribal chief, or what have you. Of course, I've no doubt the food must've taken some getting used to, and having to adjust oneself to the sight of shrunken heads and whatnot, but nevertheless… And as for me, I adapted surprisingly quickly to being the child of an absentee mother. You see, she was never really there even when she was there – if you see what I mean. Between her committees and her parties and her liaisons with her large Micronesian lover, not to mention her overall abhorrence of motherhood and human offspring in general, well…there wasn't much left to pine for. It all seemed quite natural at the time. Just my life, really. (*Beat.*) I did have a teeny bit of a breakdown, but not so's you'd have noticed.

FELICITY

(Monologue 1)

Age range: 20s – 60s

From the play *The Man Who Liked Dick*, included in the collection *A Ballyhoo in Blighty*.

Having just finished throwing a small soirée for their new neighbors with whom she was less than impressed, Felicity, a rather caustic, imperious woman by nature, is discovered here chiding her husband, Douglas, for inviting them over in the first place.

While this monologue might appear more apt for a woman in her mid-30s and upward based on the number of years Felicity's been married, it could quite easily be performed by a woman in her 20s simply by adjusting that number down.

A bore? If it were simply a matter of finding them boring, Douglas, I'd have glided through the evening on autopilot. Without wishing to sound immodest, seventeen years of marriage to you has turned me into something of an Olympian at coping with boredom. But it was all the rest of it. I mean, really…where does one begin? Aside from the fact that they were both as dull as dishwater, they were wearing matching ugly sweaters, their manners were rudimentary at best, his voice had an irritating nasal twang, she obviously believes that less is more when it comes to hair care, their persistent attempts at humour made my throat sore from having to continually employ my professional laugh, he kept picking at something at the base of his scalp that I'd rather not contemplate, she kept pushing her hair back behind her ears as if she were about to be photographed at any second, and when I asked them if they liked the vol-au-vent his eyes glazed over and she looked at me as if I were speaking Swahili. (*Beat.*) I just don't understand why you would've invited people like that into this house. And how can people like that possibly afford to buy a place identical to ours? It makes me feel cheap and underprivileged. (*Beat.*) It's going to take me weeks to alienate them.

JOY

(Monologue 1)

Age range: 20s – 50s

From the play *Kitchen Sink Drama*.

Judgmental and often brutally forthright, Joy doesn't exactly live up to her name, yet somehow her self-possession, style and level-headedness lend her a certain admirable charm. Here she has just arrived – a little later than she would have liked – at the home of her distraught sister who had recently left her a fretful message on her cell phone voicemail.

An increasingly rapid-fire delivery would probably serve this monologue well.

Darling, my apologies, you must forgive me, but it's Wednesday, as you know – the day I have to take Stephen's brats to the park – hideous, I know, but what can you do? And so there I am, sitting on this hideously uncomfortable wooden bench that's covered in lichen and bird shit, being subjected to the most appalling high-pitched squeals and laughter emanating from those pre-pubescent monsters from Stephen's squalid little pre-me marriage, wondering what the hell I'd done to deserve it all, when I attempt – in desperation – to make contact with the outside world and check my messages, and wouldn't you know it…the damned phone's out of juice. So, then I have to drag these two creatures, kicking and screaming needless to say, to the nearest wine bar where I can plug in and recharge – me and the bloody phone

– them crying and sobbing the whole three hours, of course –
even though I'd bought them more magazines and fizzy
drinks than you could possibly imagine – until I finally get a
signal, got your hideous message, unloaded the brats back
onto Stephen and charged over here as if my life depended
on it. So how are you, darling? Well, obviously you're feeling
completely hideous – but, I mean, other than that? Is
everything all right?

EILEEN

(Monologue 1)

Age range: 30s – 60s

From the play *WYWH*, included in the collection *Going Solo: One-Act Plays for One Actor.*

Since the disappearance of her young son a number of years ago, Eileen has become something of a recluse. However, since her recent foray into the world of chat rooms and online dating, life has become a lot more interesting and a lot less lonely.

A warm, friendly, and good-humored woman, Eileen, as written in the play, is in her mid-fifties. There is nothing in the text here, however, to prevent a younger actor from tackling this monologue. The one expletive here can simply be replaced with the word "eff" without losing any of the humor of their exchange.

I've been learning another language. There's no end to the challenges I'm taking on these days. Though this one still gets me a bit flummoxed at times, I have to confess. It's the language of the internet, and though it might seem simple in theory, it's actually quite tricky until you get the hang of it. I'm getting better, but Rocky – my online boyfriend – says I'm still a WIT. That's Wordsmith in Training. I was LOL when I read that…that's Laughing Out Loud, in case you didn't know. (*Beat.*) Anyway, I'm getting the hang of it, even if I do make the odd slip up, like last week when Rocky wrote and told me he'd just reached his one year anniversary of being clean and sober. He'd had a bit of a drinking problem in his past, apparently. Well, naturally I just felt so happy and thrilled for him, so I quickly typed back "So thrilled for you!!!" which I shorthanded as STFU – thinking he'd get my drift – followed by three exclamation points. Some time later a sad face appeared on my screen, followed by the words "Shut the fuck up???" followed by three question marks. Oh, I just felt so awful I could have died on the spot. It certainly taught me a lesson about making up your own shorthand. Go by the rules – the rules of the road. After I'd written back to explain what I'd meant he sent me back another emoticon of a big, beaming happy face that was wearing sunglasses, and next to it a pair of big red lips with the word "Muah" written beneath it, which he's already explained to me to be the sound you make when you blow someone a kiss. Like this… (*Pursing her lips, she demonstrates making the sound.*) Muah! (*Beat.*) It was ever so touching. Funny how you can feel so attached to someone who isn't really there, isn't it?

ACTOR 2

Age range: 20s – 40s

From the play *The Craft*, included in the collection *The Meta Plays*.

With The Craft the set-up is a little different from the norm. Two actors are performing in a play within the play – in this case a staid old romantic potboiler. But, while their physical movements and expressions are in keeping with the roles they're playing, it is their inner dialogues that we actually hear them speaking, rather than the words from the play they're performing in. And, as you will see, ACTOR 2 isn't exactly enamored with her scene partner.

Some physical movement at the beginning, as suggested by the text, would probably serve you well here, adding some visual interest and context.

I run across the stage, desperately seeking the whereabouts of my one true love...even though I can see him sitting right there and would have to be half blind not to have spotted him immediately...but...this is theatre, so on I search, hoping, hoping, until...oh yes, there he is...my heart's desire...in the form of one of the most obnoxious and egotistical jerks I've ever had the misfortune of working with. I smile sweetly. (*Beat.*) So...you want to know my terrible secret, do you? All right, I'll tell you. It's an almost uncontrollable desire to see you stripped naked and strung up by your balls from the light rigging, with a large prop of my choosing rammed up that vain, self-important and utterly talentless asshole of yours. But...since that's unlikely to transpire and not actually in the text, I suppose I'd better stick with the scripted version. (*Beat.*) After I've finished, I pause briefly, looking into his eyes to see if my words have been met with pity or loathing. (*Beat.*) As it turns out, it's neither. It's that same vacant, idiotic expression he wears every time the director gives him a note – he tries to pretend he's understood, but in truth just looks lobotomized. And his parents, with the benefit of hindsight, would probably agree with me now that that might have been the best option.

PEGGY

(Monologue 1)

Age range: 20s – 50s (Cross-castable)

From the play *Big Girl*, included in the collection *Going Solo: One-Act Plays for One Actor*.

Peggy is smart, sardonic, and in possession of a wickedly acerbic sense of humor. She also, despite her mocking self-deprecation, exudes a hard-won strength and confidence. In the source play she's a considerably overweight younger woman, but since neither age nor body size factor into this particular monologue, those considerations need not apply.

I think self-hatred is vastly underrated, don't you? I mean, everyone seems to have such a negative view of it. But if you really think about it, it makes life so much easier in so many ways. For a start, you don't have to bother giving yourself all those tiresome confidence-building pep talks inside your head every time you look in the mirror or step outside the front door. You can simply hate what you see before you, shrug your shoulders and get on with your business. And if someone insults you or shoots you a disdainful glare, it doesn't sting or chip away at your delicately crafted shell of self-confidence – it just lands harmlessly in that boggy pit of everything you already despise anyway, and fizzles out with barely a flicker. You don't wrestle with it, you just absorb it. It can save an awful lot of time in this fast-paced world of ours. Think about it. (*Beat.*) Anyway, I have to go. I have a date. (*She turns to leave, then stops and looks back over her shoulder with a wry smile.*) Yes...even me.

JOY

(Monologue 2)

Age range: 20s – 50s

From the play *Kitchen Sink Drama*.

For someone with a name like Joy, she certainly doesn't seem to spread much of it around. Blunt, unfiltered and hypercritical, she cuts a decidedly intimidating figure. But it would be a mistake to write her off as merely some sort of harridan. Her delivery may be brutally frank, but her advice is well-intentioned, and where others might perceive insensitivity, she sees only level-headed pragmatism.

Here she's found "consoling" her sister, who's concerned that her husband might be having an affair.

Look, darling, your husband's only human, after all – hard to imagine sometimes, but there you are. And more to the point, he has needs along with the rest of us – though frankly, that's even harder to imagine. But for God's sake stop going on like some button-downed hausfrau. Just stop for a second, take a deep breath, and have a good hard look at yourself: You're of a certain age; you and Graham have been married for…God knows how long; presumably you no longer find each other sexually appealing – and on the odd occasion you feel obliged to do so, it's more than likely forced and horrid; there's doubtless very little left in that burnt out ember of love that, with great force of mind, I can only vaguely imagine you once shared; and what little conversation you continue to exchange is almost certainly argumentative and combative, or else so dull and predictable that both of you have trouble summoning the energy to respond, since you both already assume to know what the other's going to say before the sentence has hardly begun. So what do you expect? These things are going to happen, darling. He's just scratching an itch, that's all. You know men and sex – it's like going to the lavatory – they'll do it just about anywhere when the urge is strong enough.

JAN

Age range: 20s – 60s (Cross-castable)

From the play *A Stunning Confession*, included in the collection *Arcane Acts of Urban Renewal: Five One-Act Comedies*.

In A Stunning Confession, a seemingly ordinary married couple settles down for the evening in front of their television. Jan, a rather high-strung, excitable woman, has spotted an actress on the screen she thinks she recognizes and is attempting to jog her husband's memory into remembering her name. In its original form the words are written to convey a clear cockney accent, but I have removed that here to allow it to be spoken in any accent. She's also described in the play as being middle-aged, but since nothing in the text below suggests that, the age range is open.

Look…it's her…what's her name? You know…her! *Her!* She was in that…that film…with that actor – the short one with the…the dark hair. Oh, you know. She played an expensive prostitute and he was…well, I don't know what he was, really…a doctor, I think…or a chemist. Or was he a fishmonger? He wore a white coat, whatever he was. Least, I think he did? (*Beat.*) Or am I thinking of something else? No, no, that's definitely the one. You know – where she was in love with him, but he wasn't in love with her, but she decided to confess her love to him anyway, but he told her he didn't have any feelings for her and he went and married someone else, and she cried and cried and almost had a nervous breakdown, and then he discovered he didn't love his wife after all, but he did still have feelings for her, so he went to her and told her how he felt, but she was still hurt, so she told him she didn't love him anymore, so he went back to his wife, and then she cried and cried and went to his work and told him she did love him really, and then he cried and said he couldn't understand how he'd let her slip through his hands in the first place, and so he got divorced and they had a big wedding, and then she got pregnant and had a baby, but it died soon after she had it, so she...she...that's all I remember.

FELICITY

(Monologue 2)

Age range: 20s – 60s

From the play *The Man Who Liked Dick*, included in the collection *A Ballyhoo in Blighty*.

Felicity and her husband have been entertaining their new neighbors, Dick and his wife, with a little welcoming party. Later, when Felicity and Dick are left alone together, Dick implies that something untoward had recently taken place between himself and her husband in a local park, prompting the abrasive, disdainful Felicity to vent her anger and disgust over her husband's behavior.

When I think of how I ran around here like a madwoman this evening, trying to prepare the vol-au-vent in time, while all the while he was secretly rubbing his hands together at the prospect of a night's prurient entertainment at my expense, it...it makes my blood boil! (*Beat.*) Not that I begrudge you and your lovely wife our little welcoming soiree, not at all. It was the least we could have done. But when I consider the sordid satisfaction that sleazy little voyeur was getting off on as he watched the whole perverted charade play out before him, I...well, it crosses a line, it truly does. I think even someone like you would have to agree with that. (*Beat.*) Not that I'm all that surprised really. His mother was well known in private circles for her moral slippage. And his father – assuming that he was – was equally notorious for inserting himself into...well, let's just say private circles.

MRS. FLAGG

Age range: 30s – 60s

From the play *A Private Practice*.

Mrs. Flagg, on the surface at least, is a somewhat guileless, unsophisticated creature whose crumbling self-image has compelled her to seek out the services of a psychiatrist. We find her here explaining to the doctor the rather extraordinary circumstances that led to the death of her first husband. The play the monologue is taken from, A Private Practice, is an out-and-out farce, and consequently the humor is of the broader variety. Remember, however, that all good farce works best when performed with utmost sincerity and conviction.

Well, I suppose there's no harm in telling you. You see, my first husband, Lance, was a guinea pig for penile implants. He was on the cutting edge of technology – much like yourself, I suppose. But they were early days and not all the wrinkles had been ironed out. Anyway, one evening, while he was watching the swimsuit segment of the Miss World contest, I heard a bloodcurdling scream coming from the living room – turned out his device had malfunctioned and impaled him to the back of the sofa! *(With a quavering voice.)* By the time the ambulance arrived it was all over. *(Dabbing her eyes with a tissue.)* Awful, it was…just awful. The manufacturers were very understanding, of course. They awarded me a lump sum of considerable size and a new, brand name three-piece sectional. No rubbish, mind you – top quality plush. Lovely to the touch, too. *(With a sigh.)* Yes, I'm afraid Lance paid a very stiff price for his pioneer spirit.

EYDIE

Age range: 30s – 60s

From the play *A Familiar Face*, included in the collection *Arcane Acts of Urban Renewal: Five One-Act Comedies*.

A human head preserved inside a large glass canister is the subject of discussion for the two ladies in A Familiar Face, a strange artifact that one of them, Dora, discovered buried in the cupboard under her stairs. Here, as they try to determine its mysterious identity, Eydie, Dora's supportive but pragmatic friend, finds herself going off on something of a tangent. As with the previous monologue taken from this collection, the original cockney accent has been largely removed to accommodate all speech patterns. Also, although a certain level of maturity may be gleaned from the text, it's not enough to warrant confining it to the character's original age range, so it's been opened up here. And as we know, death is far from being the sole purview of the elderly.

No, no, I was gonna say, doesn't look much like your Albert. Not that I saw much of him towards the end, mind. But, truth to tell, I don't recall him having such a lovely set of teeth…all due respect to him, and that. Mind you, Dora, they can work wonders these days – miracles. You'd never have recognized our Pauline in her casket. Looked like a beauty queen! I remember thinking to myself at the time – and I know it's wrong, Dora, I know it's wrong – but I thought to myself, "Well, Pauline, what a pity you couldn't of made the effort to look like that when you was with your Malcolm, 'cause if you had, he'd have probably never run off like he did." (*Beat.*) As a matter of fact, Dora – and you mustn't tell no one this, mind, not a soul – but I even thought of phoning him up and asking him for a few tips. Well, I mean, why not? It's amazing what they can do. And he obviously knows his way around a mascara brush and a compact…more than I do, anyhow. (*Beat.*) Well, they have proper training, don't they?

MRS. ANNA

(Monologue 1)

Age range: 20s – 60s (Cross-castable)

From the play *The End of the World.*

This monologue inhabits the darker side of the comedy spectrum, and coming from a play that deals with death and the afterlife, that shouldn't come as a surprise. Mrs. Anna, a firm, businesslike woman with a derisive attitude, runs a bed and breakfast establishment, and we find her here admonishing a couple of her tenants. In the play she's described as being of indeterminate nationality, but who speaks with an accent that is suggestive of being Scandinavian in origin. Whether or not you choose to inflect this piece with such an accent is entirely up to you, as I think it works perfectly well without it. She's also described as being of middle age, but nothing in the text here indicates that, so the age range is open.

You Western bourgeois pigs, always with the sense of entitlement. Me, me, I, I. You make me sick, the lot of you. You're my least favourite. My God, if you took the time to look at yourselves for one second – just one! – you'd be disgusted by your own image. You think you are so clever but you are stupid. Stupid and ignorant. You think yourselves so advanced because you can upload pictures of your precious little doggies on your telephones, when the fact is most of you think Tbilisi is something you put on a cracker. You disgust me, prancing around with those phones stuck to your heads, speaking mindless babble to people who don't care what you say, just that you say it so they can nod and answer back in their desperation to feel like they matter. Your self-obsession knows no limits. It's repulsive. It makes me sick to think of you – sick to my stomach. (*Beat.*) Perhaps if one day you drank the vomit from the glass of your own incessant introspection you might wake up and feel like a human being instead of one of your two-dimensional creations from your Madison Avenues that needs a pill to have an erection, have an opinion, or to counteract the effects of actually being alive.

EILEEN

(Monologue 2)

Age range: 30s – 60s

From the play *WYWH*, included in the collection *Going Solo: One-Act Plays for One Actor.*

The warm, friendly, and good-humored Eileen has also become something of a recluse of late. However, she's recently discovered a new life in the virtual world, and going under the screen name "Misti" she's been exploring the realm of chat rooms and online dating. While of more mature years in the original play, there's nothing here to prevent a younger actor from taking on the role.

About a month after Rocky and I had started online dating he asked if I'd send him a picture of myself, as he was curious to know what I looked like. This threw me into a bit of a panic, I don't mind telling you, as I'd…well, I'd…I may have said certain things to him regarding my age, looks, and body-type that weren't entirely accurate. But then I had a flash of inspiration. I decided that since my online persona "Misti" was my creation in the first place, I had every right to create her "look." So I Googled a few images of other people's family snapshots until I came upon an attractive young woman that seemed just right. She was sitting at a table, her head gently resting against her hand, with a pretty, sweet smile that just seemed so warm and inviting. "*That* is Misti," I said to myself. After I'd sent it to him I anxiously awaited his response. And waited…and waited. This was not like him.

His normal response time was far, far quicker than this. Something was wrong. I suddenly felt very self-conscious. Was my Misti so very different than the one he'd been imagining? Was I not his type? Should I have sent a picture that showed more skin? My Misti was wearing a turtleneck sweater, it's true, but it was a very nice one and went ever so well with her hair coloring. Still I waited. (*Beat.*) At long last his reply came through. With my heart in my mouth I read over what he had to say, the realization of my mistake and the cause of his trepidation soon becoming very apparent. He said I looked beautiful, far prettier than he'd ever imagined. He also said I looked like someone who was a truly loving, caring person. "But," he added, "and please don't take this as anything more than a casual observation, but I did happen to notice that the chair you're sitting in is a wheelchair." (*Throwing her hands in the air in incredulity.*) Why had I not seen this? "Not only that," he continued, "but I also happened to notice that through the doorway to the left of the picture you can see a staircase, and I happened to notice that the staircase is equipped with a stairlift, so I was just wondering – and again, it's nothing more than idle curiosity – but I just wondered if…well…are you a paraplegic? (*Turning away in dismay.*) What had I done? I'd ruined everything. Why had I not noticed these things? Oh, what a mess!

MRS. PENNINGTON-SOUTH

Age range: Late 30s – 50s

From the play *Suburban Redux*.

Imperious and charming in equal measure, Mrs. Pennington-South is a larger-than-life character who commands the attention of everyone in her orbit. In this monologue she's explaining to her college-aged son how she'd raised him in the hope that he was homosexual, thus sparing him from a life of stifling suburban conventions that had plagued her own. Remember, however, that although the language here is heightened, it would be a mistake to play it too over-the-top, as Mrs. Pennington-South believes passionately in every word she's saying.

It suddenly struck me – you were...oh, I don't know...three, I think – and I'd just been watching one of those gritty documentary programmes on BBC 2...the ones where, rather than feeling enlightened, I just end up feeling guilty for being me. Anyway, this particular one happened to be about homosexuality and how it could all be a result of your genes or molecules, or some such thing. And that's when it hit me. That's when I saw a little chink of light in all of that darkness. It occurred to me that perhaps...perhaps there was a way out for you, after all. Perhaps you weren't fated to replay this moribund existence that we'd all been embalmed in. (*Placing her hands to her face.*) Oh...how I wracked my brains, searching, praying for some beacon of hope within the bosom of our bloodline. There was your aunt Millicent, of course, who'd run off to Tangiers with her housekeeper and precious little else. But that had been generally ascribed by most as a matter of pure domestic necessity – especially in an under-developed country. And then, in a moment of inspired joy, I recalled your cousin Aubrey, with his penchant for strolling in the park after dark, and his overall lack of interest in the feminine gender. Oh, how I clutched to that image. I prayed, with *all* the religious fervor I could muster – which, admittedly, wasn't much – that that would be *your* destiny, too. I *wanted* that for you. I wanted that *so* badly.

PEGGY

(Monologue 2)

Age range: 20s – 50s

From the play *Big Girl*, included in the collection *Going Solo: One-Act Plays for One Actor*.

Peggy is considerably overweight. She's also smart, sardonic, and equipped with a wickedly acerbic sense of humor. Yet despite her frequent cynical and self-loathing comments, she is a strong woman in full possession of herself. While body size will be a factor to some degree when considering whether to perform this monologue, age should not be. In the original play she is portrayed as a younger woman, but with no age-related information included here the age range can be extended. Also note that the "236 pounds" mentioned here should obviously be replaced with whatever figure is pertinent to the performer.

She's found here discussing a recently purchased self-help book.

(*Declaratively.*) I weigh 236 pounds and I love every God given one of them. (*Pause.*) I don't, actually. Not if I were being honest. But that's what you're supposed to repeat, according to the instructions in the book. (*Beat.*) It's called, "The Bigger the Better." It's meant to empower you, apparently – repeating this mantra. They suggest standing completely naked in front of a full-length mirror beneath overhead lighting and repeating at least twenty times before going to bed, "I weigh 236 pounds and I love every single God given one of them." Not that it says "236" of course. It just leaves a blank space for you to plop in whatever it is you're lugging around. Then you're supposed to wake up the next morning feeling completely at peace with your physical being and the world in which it moves...or lumbers...or words to that effect. Whatever the case, it's not working. I'm not sure if it's because I hate my body or I don't believe in God...though I suspect the latter. At any rate, I've a feeling I was had. (*Beat.*) As Nietzsche so adroitly put it, "Does wisdom perhaps appear on the earth as a raven which is inspired by the smell of carrion?" (*Beat.*) Perhaps yes, perhaps no...but I did buy the book. (*Pause.*) Maybe I'll write a book someday. I'd title it: "How to Hate Your Bloated Carcass, Yet Still Continue to Enjoy a Relatively Happy, Healthy and Productive Life...Barring One or Two Exceptions...Especially When Sitting Alone on a Saturday Night with a Bottle of Vodka and a Bellyful of Bile." Or something like that. (*Beat.*) I think I'd need an editor.

MRS. ANNA

(Monologue 2)

Age range: 20s – 60s (Cross-castable)

From the play *The End of the World.*

Another darkly humorous monologue from the redoubtable Mrs. Anna, who runs an unconventional bed and breakfast establishment in the afterlife. Here she's found giving a rundown of the house rules to her newest tenant in her typical brusque, no-frills manner. As mentioned before, in the play she's described as being of indeterminate nationality, but who speaks with an accent that is suggestive of being Scandinavian in origin. Whether or not you choose to inflect this piece with such an accent is entirely up to you, but it works perfectly well without one. She's also described as being of middle age, but since nothing in the text here would indicate that, the age range is open.

Rent's due every Friday by 7:00pm at the latest, no excuses. If you have excuses, you can relay them to me as you're walking out the door with your bags. A traditional English breakfast is served every morning, Monday through Friday, at 7:30am sharp. It will consist of – though by no means restricted to, and subject to change – bacon, scrambled eggs, fried tomatoes, sausages – when in season – toast, marmalade, a variety of jams – country of origin not specified due to international sanctions – tea, freshly squeezed orange juice or artificial substitute – which in some cases may induce headaches, nausea, stomach cramps, or intestinal bleeding, and should be followed up by a consultation with your primary care giver – and, last but not least, a bottomless coffee pot. I don't care what you do behind the closed doors of your room because it's none of my business. Practice whatever religion makes you feel more complete and comfortable in your skin, and have sexual relations with whomever or whatever satiates your desires. I do, however, draw the line at white supremacy rituals, cults that involve human or animal sacrifice, kiddie porn, the importing of sex slaves from Eastern Europe and the Philippines, and unhygienic personal habits that could endanger the health and well-being of your fellow residents. (*Beat.*) I've had allsorts here over the years – every type, shape, color you could possibly imagine – and they've all been welcome. But I won't stand for any nonsense. Those are the rules, house rules, and if you don't want to play by them you can go it alone. (*Beat.*) Oh, and one more thing. Now that you're here – and for what it's worth – welcome to The End of the World.

COMEDIC MONOLOGUES

Male

ACTOR 1

(Monologue 1)

Age range: 20s – 40s

From the play *The Craft*, included in the collection *The Meta Plays*.

In The Craft the set-up is a little different from the norm. Two actors are performing in a play within the play – in this case a staid old romantic potboiler. But, while their physical movements and expressions are in keeping with the roles they're playing, it is their inner dialogues that we actually hear them speaking, rather than the words from the play they're performing in. ACTOR 1 has a decidedly cocky, narcissistic demeanor that, perhaps not surprisingly, masks the frustrated, insecure actor within. Here he steps onto the stage in character to perform his opening scene, then awaits the arrival of his scene partner.

Act Two, Scene Three. I enter from stage right…nervous but in character, cross to the chair placed downstage center, next to the small table, and sit. I look up, seemingly forlorn, and begin my brief soliloquy that speaks of the turmoil and heartache inside of me that was all-too-obviously telegraphed in the previous scene. (*Beat.*) I direct it to the fourth wall, as if speaking to anyone and no one, *and yet*…some woman in the third or fourth row is wearing a blouse of a color so loud and garish that I find my peripheral vision is being constantly distracted by it, thus diminishing the gravitas of what I'm attempting to impart to the audience at large. God I hate her – she's really screwing this up for me. (*Beat.*) I ignore her as best I can and concentrate on the words. Okay, I'm done. God, I hate her – she really threw me off. (*Beat.*) I think my expression at the end really got them, though…despite the distraction of Coco the Clown in row C or D or wherever the hell she is. (*Beat.*) All right then, darling, let's be having you…make your entrance please…*now*. (*Beat.*) Christ, where is she? Come on, come on! (*Beat.*) All right, don't panic. Try to look deep in thought, as if there's a very important inner dialogue raging inside of you – then maybe the audience will think it's all deliberate. (*Beat.*) God, I could strangle her right now! *Where the hell is she?*

HORATIO

(Monologue 1)

Age range: 20s – 50s

From the play *The Most Interesting Man in the Whole Wide World.*

Horatio Higgins, a mercurial loner with delusional disorder, has just recently been made unemployed. Here he's recounting the unfortunate chain of events that led up to his current predicament.

I ask you, how can you fire someone for being overly diligent? It makes no sense. It defies reason. They should have given me a pay raise. A slap on the back at the very least. All I got was a slap in the face. (*Beat.*) I'd seen it all before, of course. The corporate greed, the scandals, the public inquiries, the mighty falling, the jail terms, the celebrity whistle-blowers, the rotting, maggot-ridden underbelly of capitalism gone berserk. I'd seen it all. So I knew. When the time came I knew what I had to do. And I did it. I knew the risks…and still I did it. (*With damning intonation.*) Two DHL packages sent from the Chief Executive Officer to a member of his own family with no remittance, no official coding, and no apologies. Pure, unmitigated big-business sleaze. So, naturally, I took it to the CFO. His response? A big fat dismissive nothing. Yet another milk-starved minion sucking at the big nipple. So I did the only thing my conscience would allow me to do. I strode right into the corner office and confronted the all-powerful tit himself. I was nervous, I admit it. But I knew I carried with me the principled hearts and minds of 1,357 co-workers who I knew would be behind me in my quest against what was clearly an egregious and completely indefensible abuse of the system by someone who netted more in personal income each year than the company actually made in profit. (*Beat.*) And what did it get me? 1,357 averted glances and an unemployment allowance that I'm still trying to figure out how to survive on. But I will, I'll do it…I'm an accountant. (*Beat.*) Or was.

ROGER

Age range: Late teens – 30s (Cross-castable)

From the play *Indigenous Peoples*, included in the collection *A Ballyhoo in Blighty*.

Roger, a perfectly sensible and quite uncomplicated young man, has embarked upon a weekend camping trip with his girlfriend, Caroline. Having just heard Caroline relay some personal experiences regarding her upbringing, he's then asked by her to relay some of his own. This he does, but as you'll see, he doesn't seem to find anything particularly interesting or unusual about them.

My childhood? Not much to tell, really. Mother was a lesbian with an innate gift for– (*Irritated.*) And please don't say "Oh" like that, as if it were something. It was nothing. It *is* nothing. She was simply a lesbian, that's all – *is* a lesbian. But in her day it didn't have the socio-political cachet that it has nowadays. It still had a certain stigma and prejudice attached to it. So, in a moment of reckless abandon, she married Father and pretended to be happy and enacted rapture in his embrace, and …and, well, hence me. Not to imply that it was all plain sailing from then on. They were completely mismatched, you see. Not just in *that* sense, but in every sense. They never fought, which was a blessing, but that was due largely to the fact that they never spoke to one another to begin with. My upbringing was placed in the muscular hands of a rather solemn woman from Bulgaria – named Sofia, oddly enough – who, herself, spoke very little, and what rare utterances she did make were in an obscure Slavic dialect that

I'm told is now all but extinct. But it made for a quiet, peaceful childhood...if a little remote. Eventually my mother's relationship with Sofia developed into one of less commercial overtones, which appeared to make Sofia far less solemn but no less taciturn, whilst Father – rather predictably – pursued dalliances with local women of a more flavorful character whose appetites were more *en rapport* with his own. I, in the meantime, came to be viewed by both as something of an embarrassing aberration resulting from a period in their lives they'd just as soon not give a second thought to. (*Beat.*) Other than that it was all as dull as dishwater.

HANK

(Monologue 1)

Age range: 20s – 60s

From the play *The End of the World*.

The End of the World is set predominantly in a bed and breakfast establishment located somewhere in the afterlife. While there, the play's protagonist, Valentine, meets a number of singularly unorthodox visitors and fellow guests. Here he's confronted by Hank, a swaggering, bigger-than-life Texan who's trying to convince him to invest in an unusual business venture he's working on. In the original play, Hank is described as middle-aged, but with nothing in the text here to signify that, the age range is open.

Okay, I'm just gonna spell it out for ya. I think it's pretty clear that in this day and age most everyone wants to talk and no one wants to listen – specially if you're the type to bore the pants off a herd o' chickens. It's a basic, fundamental human need to be heard that we all share but no one gives a shit about. Am I right? And that's a demographic – a discontented demographic – and a market share ripe for the pluckin'. Right? So here's the answer: We take people like you – nice enough in themselves, but kinda bland on the whole…and they know it – these are smart, self-aware people, mind you – and we offer them, at an affordable price, the opportunity of having one of our medically certified surgeons – fully indemnified, mind you – implant a small plasma TV screen into their foreheads that can receive real-time feeds from some of the most popular cable television networks available, right there into that useless empty space above their eyebrows. (*Beat.*) Imagine it: You're just itchin' to impart all the tedious details of everything that's hangin' heavy on your mind to one of your co-workers at happy hour in the local bar. They're bracin' themselves for an hour or two of clenched teeth and thinkin' to themselves, "Won't he ever shut the hell up," when suddenly, to their great surprise and delight, you produce a convenient palm-sized remote control that gives them the freedom to choose between all the latest news from CNN, up-to-the-minute action from ESPN, or a thought provoking costume drama from your very own BBC, all at the touch of a button. Meanwhile, you – all too aware of just how disinterested your petty life concerns are to your captive audience – can feel free to yak yourself into a frenzy as you bask in the fully committed and rapt attention of your recipient's gaze. It's a win-win situation!

REAMS

(Monologue 1)

Age range: 40s – 60s

From the play *A Slip of the Tongue*, included in the collection *Arcane Acts of Urban Renewal: Five One-Act Comedies.*

Mr. Reams is a partner in the solicitors firm of Reams and Ramsbottom. As you might have guessed, this is a play that contains a lot of cheeky innuendo, all of which originates from the lascivious and predatory Mr. Reams and is directed at his nervous young assistant, Miss Perkins. Here he's found impressing upon her, in his customary manner, the company's expectations of its employees.

Though I've suggested an age range in the 40s to 60s, it could conceivably be pulled off by a younger actor, as long as the delivery is imbued with a strong sense of maturity and officiousness. This monologue would be particularly suitable for someone auditioning for a farce or similar works of broad comedy.

I'm afraid as the years advance, Miss Perkins, the rest of me sometimes has a little trouble keeping up. Not every part, of course. There are parts of me that can still keep it up for…well, for as long as circumstances require. The truth is, Miss Perkins, I remain a very potent force when it comes to the ins and outs of Reams and Ramsbottom, as I hope you will have the pleasure of discovering for yourself. I may no longer resemble a young stallion, Miss Perkins, but I can still extend myself in a number of surprising areas…when I see

43

the right openings. Furthermore, we here at R & R pride ourselves on presenting valuable employment opportunities for firm-breasted…or, or that is to say, firm-*minded* young people with a desire to give…or rather, to, to, to *get* ahead. You must realize, Miss Perkins, that when someone adopts a Reams and Ramsbottom position we expect them to display to us everything that that position would imply. We expect our staff to bend over backwards and show us just what it is that they have to offer. This is a man's world, Miss Perkins, as I'm sure you will have discovered, which is why we here at R & R have always prided ourselves on our unstinting support and encouragement of female openings. I'd strongly advise you not to squander this golden opportunity.

BOB

Age range: 20s – 60s (Cross-castable)

From the play *The Skewed Picture*, included in the collection *The Meta Plays*.

In The Skewed Picture, the intellectually curious Bob has just become aware of the concept of a parallel universe, which he excitedly shares with his wife, Betty. Questioning whether their living room wall (the fourth wall on stage) is, perhaps, not just a wall but a portal to another dimension, he begins to hypothesize as to who might be on the other side and why they might be watching them.

If in fact, as I'm becoming increasingly convinced, this is not really a wall at all but a quantum event, then what we see before us could actually function as some sort of inter-universe two-way mirror. Just imagine…right now, right as we speak, there could be someone – hell, there could be a whole bunch of people – just sitting there, staring at us. And perhaps in observing us – in studying us – they're hoping to see something of themselves in us, and consequently find a sort of catharsis in our shared experience. I think they're hoping to learn things from us that they can take away and apply to their own lives in their own universe. (*Beat.*) I wouldn't be surprised if many of these people are gazing at us in search of some form of…edification. They're probably all sophisticates and aesthetes with a hankering for the lofty. They wouldn't be looking for cheap entertainment or silly distractions. These poor people are probably *desperate* for some sort of meaningful cultural experience – I can almost feel it oozing from them. They're starved and they're looking to us for nourishment. (*With ever-increasing fervor*) And damn it, Betty, we're going to do everything within our power to make sure they get it. Yes, we are. We're going to give them all of the culture they'd ever dreamed of and more besides. We'll read the classics to them, every one of them; we'll recite poetry from Keats to Cummings; we'll play them Brahms and Beethoven; we'll re-enact every play ever written in any language. We'll sing operas to them; we'll show them our dance steps; we'll read them every thought of every philosopher that ever existed; we'll give them lectures in art history and seminars on mime. By God, Betty, by the time we're done with them, they'll be on their knees, *begging* for a way to thank us!

HORATIO

(Monologue 2)

Age range: 20s – 50s

From the play *The Most Interesting Man in the Whole Wide World*.

Horatio Higgins, a mercurial loner with delusional disorder, frequently regales the people he meets with spurious, fantastical tales of his life and times. Here he is found recounting to his new female friend the tragic circumstances that led up to the death of his mother and father.

My parents, I'm afraid, were taken from me before their time. Quite tragically. Horribly, in fact. You see, they worked for the World Wildlife Fund – both of them. They just loved nature, what can I say? They'd dedicated their lives to it…literally, as it turned out. He was a photographer, she a documentarian, as it were. On that last, fatal assignment they'd embedded themselves in a far-flung and little known corner of Papua New Guinea in search of an exotic variety of slug that had previously been ruled extinct by the powers that be. But they were determined to prove its existence by unearthing the last remaining specimens. Unfortunately for them that particular part of the country was also home to a race of vicious, pigmy-like creatures that still practiced the culinary art of cannibalism. (*Beat.*) They never stood a chance. They were consumed almost immediately. One man's meat…is another man's parents. In that corner of the world, at least. (*Beat.*) And it wasn't easy, I will admit – continuing through life knowing that your own dear mother and father had passed through the primitive digestive system of a hitherto unknown tribe of…well, for the sake of argument we'll call them "people." Knowing that the person you once called "Mummy" – who you'd idolized and adored since your earliest memories, and who'd always taken such pride in her appearance and her public persona – had to suffer the final indignity of being shat out of the bowels of a total stranger.

ACTOR 1

(Monologue 2)

Age range: 20s – 40s

From the play *The Craft*, included in the collection *The Meta Plays*.

In The Craft, two actors are performing in a play within the play – in this case a staid old romantic potboiler. While their physical movements and expressions are in keeping with the roles they're playing, it is their inner dialogues that we actually hear them speaking, rather than the words from the play they're performing in. Here, the surly, arrogant ACTOR 1 waits as his scene partner finishes her monologue, sharing with us – via his inner dialogue – his thoughts on agents, his costar, and the play they're acting in as he does so.

I wonder if there's any agents in the audience tonight. I invited six but none of them responded. Wait a second…that guy back there with the glasses looks like he might be. (*Beat.*) On second thoughts, no…too hip. Useless bastards. I expect they were all "too busy." Yeah, too busy propping up some bar, getting wasted after a hard day's skimming cash off the backs of their clients' hard work. Parasites. They should be sat out there doing their job…scouting for talent…witnessing art. (*Beat.*) Oh, look out – her big speech is about to end. And not before time. She milks that thing like a Jersey cow. (*Beat.*) And if there *are* any agents out there tonight, I hope they're taking note, because *this* is acting. Not only am I having to navigate this scene alone with Ling-Ling here, but I mean,

49

really – she had an abortion two years ago after a brief romp in the rhododendrons with the former gardener? I mean, who writes this crap? I'm supposed to be shocked and appalled by this revelation? It's hardly the stuff of Grand Guignol. Now, if she'd been raped by her father and given birth to a hideously deformed, inbred monstrosity that she kept chained to a post behind the summerhouse, *then...then* we'd have a revelation...*then* we'd have something to work with. But no, it's just your average, plain vanilla abortion saga, in response to which – and to great effect, using every skill at my disposal – I fix her with a steely gaze that betrays neither outrage nor compassion.

HORATIO

(Monologue 3)

Age range: 20s – 50s

From the play *The Most Interesting Man in the Whole Wide World.*

Horatio Higgins, a mercurial loner with delusional disorder, has recently lost his job, leaving him feeling lonely and adrift in the world. During a visit to the Job Opportunity Centre in search of new employment, however, he meets a shy, sensitive young woman named Nore, and suddenly his life takes on a whole new meaning.

I still find it hard to believe. Less than twelve hours ago I was…what's the word? Languishing. I was languishing. Knee-deep in the doldrums. Feeling small and insignificant. And now, all of a sudden, I'm…ten feet tall. Not literally, of course…but I do feel taller. (*Beat.*) Her name's Nore. As in Queen Noor, or Norway, or neither nor, or Nordic, even. Not that she looks Nordic. Anything but, in fact. Which is rather exotic in itself. Our eyes crossed…well, not crossed in the astigmatic sense, but met…whilst scanning the career notices pinned to the particleboards at the Job Opportunity Centre. Not that they had any job opportunities, but…well, what's in a name? (*Beat.*) I fell immediately. Totally. You know how you do? How you just know? Well…I knew. I couldn't tell her I was looking for a job, of course. It might've given off the wrong signals. So I told her I was scouting for job opportunities for the employees I'd just laid off. After I'd said it her eyes took on a watery appearance, as if she was

51

about to cry. When I saw that...that honest, pure, heartfelt human emotion, I did for a moment consider coming clean...surmising that she might be equally touched by my honest, open, human admittance of a small untruth. But I couldn't. I couldn't let her down. It would've been cruel. And anyway, I was touched. So I kept it up – out of duty. (*Beat.*) Anyway, we chatted for a while about this and that. Nothing too deep or personal; no religion or politics. It was our first date, after all. But even in those superficial pleasantries I could tell she was something special. A catch, if you will. So...after a while...I popped the question. Not *the* question, of course – not marriage – not at this juncture. Even so, it took all the courage I could muster – all I had – but I did it. I asked her if she would do me the honor of joining me for dinner this evening. And to my utter astonishment she said yes! (*Beat.*) Well, actually she said no. Understandably, I was crushed. Devastated, I think, would be closer to the mark. Pissed off...resigned...dead inside. And then *my* eyes took on a watery appearance, as if *I* was about to cry. And then...she said yes!

HANK

(Monologue 2)

Age range: 20s – 60s

From the play *The End of the World.*

A bed and breakfast establishment located in the afterlife is the setting for The End of the World, and while there the play's protagonist, Valentine, encounters a host of eccentric visitors and fellow guests. One of those visitors is Hank, a swaggering, bigger-than-life Texan, who's discovered here giving a rather candid, unfiltered assessment of Valentine's personality. In the original play, Hank is described as middle-aged, but with nothing in the monologue here to indicate that, the age range is open.

Okay, I'm gonna tell you this, but it's completely confidential, totally off the record, and subject to legal recrimination against not only you, but your family, your friends, and just about anyone you've ever known in your entire life, okay? Okay, here it is: You're kind of boring, right? Not bein' rude, just frank, you understand – or Hank I guess, ha, ha! – but ya come across to other people – or me, at least – as bein' a kind of a boring guy to talk to. I mean, all kinda proper and thinkin' it all through before ya speak – I mean, who has time for that, right? Do you see what I'm gettin' at? That stuff what's comin' outta your mouth ain't exactly gonna set the world on fire, is it? That ain't napalm spoutin' from your lips. It's dull – it's indecisive. It's grey, not black and white. People nowadays, they ain't got time for thinkin' and waitin' and tryin' to figure out just what the hell it is you're tryin' to get at. You gotta get that sound bite in fast or else you're dead in the water – yesterday's news. This is a world of snap decisions, snap polls, and snap judgments. Three pauses and, hey buddy, you're outta here!

MR. LOVEWORTH

Age range: 20s – 60s

From the play *Carbon-Based Life Form Seeks Similar*, included in the collection *A Ballyhoo in Blighty*.

A dating agency might seem a rather quaint concept in the digital era, but there's nothing old-fashioned about Mr. Loveworth's approach to matchmaking. Officious and forthright, he's discovered here impressing upon his new client that being yourself in this day and age simply isn't good enough.

Look, Leslie, I'm only trying to help you achieve your goals, but if I'm to do so, you're going to have to confront some uncomfortable truths. Now, in prehistoric times, things were much more straightforward. You could simply wrap yourself in a pelt, grunt a few times at your heart's desire and live happily ever after. But these days things are a little more complicated. Every aspect of your being has to be cultivated and contrived. Nothing can be left to chance. The way you dress, the way you walk, the way you smile, the way you talk, all of it has to be manufactured with absolute precision in order to create the *real* you – the one that closes the deal. Then and only then will you have become something truly viable in today's fickle and uncertain market. Let me put it this way: let's say I send you out to meet with a very nice gentleman who you find yourself very attracted to, and the next evening you anxiously await his call. He, meanwhile, that very same evening, is enjoying cocktails with friends who are all eager to hear the outcome of his first date, and to whom he relays any one of the following: "She redefined the word dull." "From the way she dressed I assumed she was manic depressive." "Her hair kept reminding me of my grandmother." "She was nice enough, but God, that annoying laugh!" Or perhaps, "In a million years I could *never* get used to that nose." (*Beat.*) Do you see what I mean? Incidentally, *your* nose – have you considered surgery?

HORATIO

(Monologue 4)

Age range: 20s – 50s

From the play *The Most Interesting Man in the Whole Wide World.*

Horatio Higgins, a mercurial loner with delusional disorder, has just recently lost his job as an accountant. Here contemplates on how he ended up in that particular line of work to begin with as well as what better use his talents might have been put to.

Don't know how that actually came about, come to think of it – becoming an accountant, that is. Not a childhood dream, it must be said. Just sort of happened, really…before I knew it. I should have been something far different, something more suited to my talents. Not that I'm not good at it – I am. One of the best. Perhaps *the* best – who knows? It's never been put to the test. But I'm an untapped resource. My potential is massive. If only people knew that. Knew the truth. But they don't – and that's the trouble. The fact is I'm wasted on budgets and number crunching. I'm so much more. I should be up to my neck in…nuclear physics and quantum leaps…genome maps, that sort of thing. Breaking down barriers, discovering new directions for the future of mankind. That's much more up my alley. (*Beat.*) Or pop singing. I'd have made a sensational pop singer. Not that I have much of a voice, if I were being honest. But you don't need it nowadays. What I do have is the off look and the attitude…and that's the clincher if you've an eye to becoming an internationally recognized, multi-platinum selling recording artiste. I could've been huge. World-class. And videos – I'd have made some groundbreaking videos. I have all sorts of ideas. They're all in my head. Even now. Had to have changed my name, of course – "Horatio Higgins" not having sufficient appeal to the all-important teen market. But everything requires sacrifice, doesn't it? That said, if you don't have the right background for these things there are very few doors that'll open up to you. *(Beat.)* I know…I've tried.

DR. PECKSNIFF

Age range: 20s – 60s

From the play *A Private Practice*.

Dr. Pecksniff, a decidedly unorthodox psychiatrist, is meeting with his new patient, Mrs. Flagg, a gullible housewife with a crumbling self-image. Seizing on her admittance of a penchant for steamy romance novels, Pecksniff attempts to convince Mrs. Flagg of her imminent slide into moral turpitude.

The play the monologue is taken from, A Private Practice, is an out-and-out farce, but keep in mind that all good farce works best when performed with utmost sincerity and conviction. Also, although Pecksniff is written as a man of more advanced years in the original play, there is no reason this monologue couldn't be performed by a younger actor, as long as the delivery is imbued with a strong sense of maturity and officiousness.

Oh, my dear lady, if you could only hear yourself. You really have no idea what's happening to you, do you? Your weakness for manipulation is quite remarkable and I must tell you, you made a very wise decision in coming here to see me today. Very wise, indeed. It's the thin end of the wedge, you see. (*Pacing the room.*) Oh, I'm sure it begins harmlessly enough – a timid toe dipped oh-so-lightly into the suggestive waters of romantic fiction. But believe me, my dear, before you know it you'll be swimming in a sea of unimaginable filth and depravity. It's a disease, Mrs. Flagg, that tempts and torments even the most chaste and pure of heart. (*Forebodingly.*) You are on the edge, Mrs. Flagg – teetering. One push and you could spiral recklessly into a world of unending mental and physical abandonment. A condition so racked by depraved thoughts and vile smelling activities that the very fibre of your existence will feel soiled. You'll look into the mirror one day and no longer see the lily-white splendour of all that is Mrs. Flagg looking back at you. Oh dear, no. I'm afraid all you'll see is the image of everything that you have become: a sweating, heaving mound of flesh, grunting and snorting like some repugnant farm animal. (*Beat.*) It's most unpleasant.

REAMS

(Monologue 2)

Age range: 40s – 60s

From the play *A Slip of the Tongue*, included in the collection *Arcane Acts of Urban Renewal: Five One-Act Comedies*.

Mr. Reams is a partner in the solicitors firm of Reams and Ramsbottom. Perhaps not surprisingly, this is a play that contains a lot of cheeky innuendo, all of which originates from the lascivious and predatory Mr. Reams and is directed at his skittish young assistant, Miss Perkins. Here he's found taking a call that delivers him some unfortunate news, which he then attempts to parlay into an assignation with his anxious aide.

Though I've suggested an age range in the 40s to 60s, it could conceivably be pulled off by a younger actor, as long as the delivery is imbued with a strong sense of maturity and officiousness.

Gerald Reams speaking…Yes, this is he…Who? (*With an air of disdain.*) Oh, yes, how are you?…No, no I'm afraid I haven't…Well, this is most unexpected, I must say…At what hour?…I see…Well, with all due respect, I cannot express in strong enough terms how inconvenient this is to my schedule…I see…Well, that's that then…Good day to you. (*He ends the call.*) That was Mrs. Reams. Apparently she will not be dining with me this evening at Le Coq Rouge – a reservation, I might add, that I have greased untold opportunistic palms in order to retain – as she has made, so I am told, alternative arrangements. (*Placing his hand on his brow.*) Oh, my, my, Miss Perkins, what an unfortunate predicament this places me in. I am now suddenly faced with the unenviable prospect of either dining alone at one of our fair city's most exclusive and discriminating restaurants, or returning home to eat a pre-packaged meal that would otherwise have been frozen for all eternity. I suddenly feel as though I'd been...cast adrift. (*Beat.*) I don't suppose...I don't suppose I could entice you, Miss Perkins, into taking a little nibble at Le Coq Rouge? You know that there's many a young underpaid secretary in London that would be willing to compromise themselves in unthinkable ways for the chance of getting a little Le Coq Rouge inside them.

HORATIO

(Monologue 5)

Age range: 20s – 50s

From the play *The Most Interesting Man in the Whole Wide World.*

Horatio Higgins is a mercurial loner with a well-rounded, though occasionally truncated intellect. He is afflicted with delusional disorder, which often manifests itself through grandiose illusions about himself and the world he inhabits. Despite this, he has, thus far, been able to live a relatively high-functioning life. We find him here having just risen from his bed and preparing to face the day ahead.

It's really quite strange when you think about it. I mean, why is it that it's only at moments like this, when I'm completely alone, with no one to hear me but me, that I begin to feel like…well, me…a complete person…the real me…the definite article, if you will? When it's just me with me I…I truly believe that I come to embody that person that deep down I know myself to be. I become that certain someone who, in all modesty, could legitimately describe themselves as an interesting person. An interesting personality. The truth is, I don't know of anyone else quite like me in the whole world. That's not to say that there isn't, but if there is I've never met them. Which, if you consider it, opens the door to the possibility that I could be…which is not to say that I am, but that I could quite possibly be…the most interesting man in the whole wide world. *(Beat.)* Then again, if it's just me that's privy to this knowledge then what exactly does that mean?

What does it matter? It could have been me who painted the Mona Lisa, but if I'd just stuck it in a drawer and never shown it to anyone, what would have been the point in painting it? Who would have known of its dark, enigmatic beauty? No one. It would never have become the celebrated masterpiece and pop culture icon that's revered by millions to this very day. (*Beat.*) Which is why I definitely made the right decision in getting out of bed this morning and presenting myself to the world at large…yet again.

EDWIN

Age range: 30s – 60s

From the play *A Private Practice*.

Edwin's wife, Gladys, has just returned home from paying a visit to a psychiatrist. During an ensuing argument, Gladys smacks Edwin across his head and storms out of the room in a fury. Here Edwin attempts to makes sense of her outburst as well as to opine on the reasons why the romantic spark in their marriage seems to have fizzled.

The play A Private Practice, from which this monologue is taken, is rooted solidly in farce, but it's worth remembering that all works in the genre of farce are most effective when performed with a high degree of truthfulness and certitude.

I don't understand. This is not like Gladys at all. Not at all. Well…hardly at all. (*Beat.*) It's that doctor, that's what it is! Upsetting her mental balance – fiddling with her mind. Yes, well, he'll have a piece of my mind before I'm finished – disrupting my marital bliss. I think it's time I paid him a little visit myself. This is domestic violence, this is. He ought to be locked up! (*Beat.*) I just hope next-doors didn't get an earful. I'll say it was the telly up loud…Miami Vice. (*Beat.*) The thing is, when she told me she was going to see a psychiatrist I thought she was having me on. It's embarrassing. No one in my family's ever been to a psychiatrist. We were normal. Well…all except great aunt Beatty, that is. But that wasn't really a psychiatrist – just one of them blokes in a white coat that takes you away. So he took her. Poor love had gone a bit funny, though. Kept wandering into the street in her bra and panties, introducing herself to passersby as Dame Barbara Cartland. (*Beat.*) "You just need to get your expectations in order, Gladys," I said. "It's not that I don't think you're an attractive woman, but you can't expect the flames of passion to burn for all eternity – that only happens in your novels." My mum and dad had separate beds for thirty years and never spoke but three words to each other from one day to the next – and they were happy…'til Mum topped herself. But, I mean, before that. (*Beat.*) Anyway, it's all a bit overrated, if you ask me. Never was much of a ladies man, to tell you the truth. More of a man's man, I'd say…even though I'm not quite sure what that means. 'Course, in my day you didn't have a choice. You were what you were. If you were a man, then you were a man, and you had to act like a man, regardless if you were a man or a man's man, 'cause a man was a man was a man, whether he was a ladies man, or a man's man, or a man's man trying to act like a ladies man, or just a man…or not. (*Beat.*) Things were a lot simpler then.

DRAMATIC MONOLOGUES

Female

RACHEL

Age range: 20s – 50s

From the play *The One-Eyed Guru.*

Rachel, an unassuming but surprisingly determined woman, has returned home at an unusually late time, where she is confronted by her husband, Jack, who has been anxiously waiting up for her. Eventually, however, it is Rachel who does the confronting, when she produces a scarf of particular significance.

The actual use of a light scarf would work well here, adding a physical dynamic at various points throughout the piece, but of course it could just as easily be mimed.

(*Proffering a scarf.*) Here, take it. It's Melanie's. (*Beat.*) Yes, Jack, Melanie's – you do remember Melanie, don't you? You work with her every day…to say the least. Surely her name must ring a bell or two? I know it's hers. I know it from that pungent smell of a Chanel No. 5 knock-off. That and the fact that I found the tail end of it poking out from beneath our bed. (*Beat.*) I've seen her wearing it often. It's obviously a favourite. Which is why I'm sure she'd be very relieved to have it returned. (*Beat.*) And no, this didn't make me feel any better, Jack…having you wait up into the night, wondering all the time where I was? Having you worry and fret about who I was with or what I was doing? Having nasty, insidious thoughts clawing their way into your mind as you tried like a fool to pretend to yourself that everything was all right? No, it didn't. Not really. (*Beat.*) But perhaps…perhaps if everybody knew but *you*, because you were too cowardly or naïve to face the obvious; perhaps if *you* had *your* friends telling you that you were being made a mockery of; perhaps if *you'd* had the phone slammed down on you a dozen times the moment your voice was heard on the other end; perhaps if *you'd* smelled cheap perfume on your husband's jacket, on his shirts, on the sheets, in the car, up your nose, always, everywhere, lined to the inside of your nostrils like some noxious chemical you couldn't escape no matter where you went, no matter what you did, then yes, *yes*...I might have felt better.

ELAINE

Age range: 20s – 50s

From the play *Kitchen Sink Drama*.

Elaine, a normally reserved, timid woman, recently had an illicit encounter with a complete stranger that has left her in a potentially life-threatening situation. Here she's found railing against the vagaries of life to her sister Joy.

In the original play, Elaine is described as being of middle age, but there is nothing in the text here to prevent a younger actor from tackling this monologue.

Risks? I don't know risks. I don't understand them. They've never been a part of my life. I just did one thing, one time – *one time* – and now I must pay for it with this. It's not fair, Joy, it's not. I don't care what you say, there's no justification for it. It's as if life was sitting there, waiting to ambush me, waiting for me to step out of line, to step outside of my little boundaries, and then...wham! And for what? Desire for another person – to *feel* another person. To connect. To feel connected to someone...*something*. For Christ's sake, Joy, at the end of the day I'm just like everyone else. And the most ridiculous part, if you want to know the honest truth, is the sex wasn't even that good – not really. But I'll tell you what did feel good: I felt wanted. I felt wanted by somebody...and that felt very good – even under those coarse, crude circumstances. And I haven't felt that in a long, long time, and...and...and that's all I can say. (*Beat. Her emotions getting the better of her.*) Except that...that...that I think everyone needs to feel that sometimes...wanted...for whatever reason. Just to remind them that...that they're someone...that they matter. Even if it's only for a couple of minutes with a stranger who doesn't really care anyway...and that...that shouldn't be a bad thing...that's all. (*Beat.*) That's all.

WOMAN

(Monologue 1)

Age range: 20s – 40s

From the play *The Replica*, included in the collection *Going Solo: One-Act Plays for One Actor*.

In this piece taken from the one-person play The Replica, an abused wife reflects on her abusive husband's increasingly nefarious conduct. The unnamed woman in question here is a stoic, contemplative sort, but with a noticeably sardonic edge.

I married Karl in a fit of existential panic, and, like most decisions made in a state of panic, it wasn't a particularly wise one. He was older and colder, and quite successful. He ran his heart, mind, and business with ruthless efficiency, and, unburdened by the need to please, he was free to treat people in whatever way would best achieve his goals, however callous the method. (*Beat.*) Soon, the success of Karl's various business ventures began to grow at an astonishing rate, as did his loathsomeness. Gradually, visits and phone calls from family and friends grew less frequent. I hardly saw Karl, so busy was he making money and enemies. My days became filled with television and tranquilizers – as prescribed by my general practitioner. I discovered that one seemed to compliment the other surprisingly well. I rarely went outside unless I had to. A quick trip to the supermarket or to get a prescription filled was all I could cope with. People always seemed to be looking at me strangely...as if they knew something I didn't. Once, the woman in the bakery told me she'd seen Karl late the other night stop his car and pick up a skinny blond boy a couple of streets away, and inquired if it was our son. I told the woman she must be mistaken, as we didn't have any children. The woman insisted it was Karl, and added that she'd seen him putting his arm around the boy, so obviously they were close. "Perhaps it was a nephew?" the woman suggested. "Perhaps it was," I replied. I stopped shopping there after that. I'd make do with sliced bread.

CHRISTINE

(Monologue 1)

Age range: 20s – 50s

From the play *The Treachery of Images.*

In The Treachery of Images, a married couple are placed in the unthinkable position of having to come to terms with the murder of their daughter. While the wife, Christine, has withdrawn into a deadened world of suppressed rage and bitterness, her husband, Tom, has taken the unusual step of publicly announcing his forgiveness of their daughter's killer, driving a profound wedge between them. Here Christine is found examining the nature of their relationship and whether what they thought they had together ever really existed.

In the original play, Christine is described as a woman of middle age, but in this particular monologue there's nothing in the text to prevent the age range from being broadened.

Ah, yes…that word again…*us.* The problem is…there's a you and a there's a me, but I don't believe that there is an *us* anymore. I sometimes wonder if there ever was. In the beginning, I suppose. But looking back…what was it? (*Beat.*) What was it really? I'm sure I thought it was love, but I wonder now if it was really just…a close approximation? Because it's all so new, isn't it, when you're starting out? So how are you supposed to know? How do you know what you're you feeling? How do you know if it's the real thing or…or just something close to it? How do you know the difference? I mean, you're innocent and naive and everything's new, and…then one day you meet someone and you find yourselves attracted to each other, and you share things in common and you make each other laugh and feel special and important in ways you'd never felt before, and it's all rather like being a little drunk. And while it's all still heady and intoxicating, you find yourselves making all kinds of plans and commitments for the future, and you're so caught up in it all that you don't even notice the buzz wearing off. It all becomes a blur of years and events, of birthdays and anniversaries, highs and lows…a lifetime. And you never stop to re-examine it…not really. Because it's done. And you're scared to. So you don't. (*Beat.*) Until something like this happens.

KLAMIDIA

Age range: 20s – 40s

From the play *Leah's Gals.*

Leah's Gals is ever-so-loosely based on the Bard's King Lear, and is equal parts cruel tragedy and broad comedy, or in other words, a tragicomedy. Matriarch Leah and her best friend have been residing with her eldest daughter, Klamidia, for quite some time now, and Klamidia – a conniving, duplicitous woman – has almost reached her breaking point.

That duplicitousness can be performed to great effect here, with the initial half of the monologue offering a spiteful rant, before pivoting sharply – right where the (Beat.) is inserted – into feigned care and concern, then back again near the very end.

If you find the Southern accent here a little challenging, feel free to iron out any of the colloquial language and phrasings into more formal English.

You wanna know what the problem is, Mama? All right, I'll tell ya flat out, right here an' now what the god damned problem is: you an' that hanger-on o' yours – or whatever she is – that's what the problem is. You've done nothin' but sit around an' drink yourselves stupid an' treat this place like a third-rate casino since ya got here. It's bad enough with you stickin' yer nose in where it ain't wanted all the time, let alone havin' yer ugly old lesbian friend messin' up the place an' fillin' up our brand new garage with all her shit. I warned you about this time an' time again, an' ya never took a blind bit o' notice. I'm tired of her crap litterin' up the place, I'm sick of her sassin' me every time she thinks I ain't listenin', an' I'm up to here with the way you two keep carryin' on 'round here, actin' like a couple o' drunken old bar hags. (*Beat.*) Listen, Mama, I just wanna do what's best for ya, that's all. A woman o' your age shouldn't be livin' her life like it was some kinda wild party. With the little time you got left, you should be slowin' it down an' takin' things easy. This woman ain't a good influence on ya, you know that, an' the sooner she's gone the better. Then maybe we can fix up the summer house for ya, put a nice big-screen TV in there, so ya can spend ya last days quietly, watchin' Oprah an' QVC an' makin' peace with yerself. It's what ya deserve, Mama. You've had a colorful life, but all I want for you now is to have a dignified an' respectable end. Your problem is yer still actin' like you're the one rulin' the roost. But ya ain't. Things are different now, an' you need to start actin' yer age an' doin' what you're told, 'cause that torch has been passed already.

THE OTHER WOMAN

Age range: 20s – 60s

An abridged version of the monologue *Organ Failure*, included in the collection *Going Solo: One-Act Plays for One Actor*.

The other woman here, of course, is one who has been having an affair with a married man – for quite some time in this instance. But that affair recently came to an end due to the passing of her lover, the circumstances of which fall into something of a morally gray area.

A sagacious woman with an acerbic edge, here she addresses his corpse which lies in a coffin before her, recounting the series of events that led up to that final, fatal moment.

I will miss you, you know. Because as awful as it is...*was*...it was what I knew. I knew it wasn't good, I knew I wanted better, but it was what I had...and I accepted it as such. But on the occasion of our last conversation...something changed. Not in you; certainly not in your voice. That was the same, slurred, barely comprehensible, self-pitying rambling I was oh so very used to. No, it was...in me. Something in me...somehow...heard you differently. The feeble, garbled plea for help was just the same. My response – dropping everything and rushing over – was just the same. But inside...inside of me...well, I guess one of my organs quit on you, too. I didn't feel a thing. (*Beat.*) You see, what you don't know is...you were still alive when I got there. (*Beat.*) I looked down at you, crumpled in a heap on the floor, battered and bruised from yet another bender session of flailing around blind drunk. You weren't conscious but you were breathing. And I thought to drag you to your bed and get you cleaned up a bit, just as always. But I didn't. I decided to sit in the chair and contemplate things – contemplate you. And the longer I stared at you, the further away you seemed. After a while it was as if I was staring at someone else. Someone I didn't know. And then you began to vomit. (*Beat.*) Your body started jerking violently as the vomit forced its way out of your mouth and nose. But you were still unconscious and breathing it back in, your throat choking on the acid, gasping for breath. And I sat in that chair watching you drown...until finally the struggling stopped and everything was quiet and still. And I waited...waited until I was sure the peace was permanent...for both of us. (*Beat.*) Then I called for help...even though neither of us needed it. Because, you see, sometimes in life...you've just got to help yourself.

LEAH

(Monologue 1)

Age range: 30s – 60s

From the play *Leah's Gals*.

Leah's Gals, a tragicomedy loosely based on King Lear, is equal parts cruel tragedy and broad comedy, and it's the former that's in evidence here. Indomitable matriarch Leah has asked her three daughters for declarations of undying love, but when her youngest daughter, Patina, refuses to do so, Leah's wrath and vitriol are unleashed upon her unsparingly.

Written as a woman of more advanced years in the original play, there's nothing in the text of this particular piece to prevent a younger actor from taking it on.

As with the other monologues taken from Leah's Gals, if you find the Southern accent here a little challenging, feel free to iron out any of the colloquial language and phrasings into more formal English.

The truth? *The truth?* You wouldn't know the truth if it walked right up to ya an' slapped ya upside the head. An' to think you was ma favorite. To think I believed you'd be the one takin' care o' me the most in the last days I got left. How could I o' been so dumb? How could I o' let myself be deceived so? By God, I rue the day I ever allowed your daddy to stick himself inside me an' spit his white venom on my eggs. I'd o' rather been raped by a monkey than have spawned such a cruel,

cold bag o' bones as you. (*Beat.*) I'll tell ya what the truth is –
the truth is I ain't yer mama! There's no blood o' mine in you.
You're all yer daddy, I see that now. He was a mistake an'
now it turns out you were, too. I shouldn't be surprised. Ya
spend one lousy night with some drunken, washed-up piece
o' nothin' – what do ya expect to come from it. All ya beget
from trash is more trash. You got about as much room for
me in your heart as ya do yer god damned cat…or the
garbage man. There ain't nothin' more worth sayin'. I only
got two daughters now – an' as far as the money's concerned,
it'll be split between the two of em'. I ain't gonna waste one
more red cent on no cuckoo that went an' made a home in
my womb. No sir, no way. (*Beat.*) Now get out – whoever you
are!

WOMAN

(Monologue 2)

Age range: 20s – 60s

From the play *The Replica*, included in the collection *Going Solo: One-Act Plays for One Actor.*

Taken from the one-person play The Replica, we're presented here with an abused wife who we find recounting her recent attempt at regaining some sense of order amid her ever-deteriorating surroundings. Though her manner is friendly and personable, it's also somewhat impassive, a result of her having become inured to her unfortunate circumstances.

The first time he hit me he seemed genuinely horrified at what he'd done. He appeared, in his anguish, and much to my surprise, to actually take a step back and re-examine himself and the person he'd become. The second time, less so. The third and thereafter it became a matter of routine. (*Beat.*) Like anything, I suppose, the more you do it the less you think about it. Familiarity breeds contempt...and contempt becomes familiar. It's all what you get used to, isn't it? (*Beat.*) Before long, I found my face to be hardening almost as fast as my heart. I thought about telling someone. I thought about a lot of things. It's all I ever seemed to do – stare out at nothing in particular...wondering if it would change. (*Beat.*) Eventually it got to the point where I'd let both myself and the house go to such an extent that even I couldn't stand it anymore. One morning, I got up and showered first thing, just like normal people did, made a little effort in my appearance – for what purpose, I wasn't quite sure, but I did it anyway – and began the task of reclaiming some sense of order out of the chaos that was now my habitat. With a zeal that surprised even me, I swept, dusted, cleaned, sorted, and organized. The bedroom, in particular, had become a shrine to neglect, and the piles of dirty clothes and discarded folderol seemed never-ending. Still, I persevered. Nearing the end of my task, I decided to make sense of the stack of business papers and printed emails that Karl routinely emptied from his briefcase onto the floor of his closet. As I stacked and tidied, I came upon a pornographic magazine filled with pictures of naked teenagers, all with Russian names. Dimitri, Vladimir, Igor, Kostya, Alek. I pushed the magazine back amongst the pile of papers as surreptitiously as I imagined Karl must've done on numerous occasions, and banished the thought of it from my mind. (*Beat.*) I'd never seen it.

CHRISTINE

(Monologue 2)

Age range: 20s – 50s

From the play *The Treachery of Images*.

After the brutal rape and murder of their daughter, a married couple must come to terms with the dreadful tragedy that has befallen them. The wife, Christine, has essentially shut down, stifled as she is by her grief, while her husband, Tom, has embraced a more reasoned, accepting approach to their plight. Those differences have now strained their relationship to its limit, and here Christine attempts to explain their situation from her perspective.

In the original play, Christine is described as a woman of middle age, but in this particular monologue there's nothing in the text to prevent the age range from being broadened.

For the life of me I can't understand it. (*Beat.*) But I need to. I *have* to. She was ours, Tom. She was yours and mine. And I feel so dead inside...dead and empty. And sometimes I...I can barely breathe, and it's in my head and in my chest and in my lungs, and it all gets tighter and tighter and I just want it all to stop, I want it all to go away and just let me die...let me out of this. (*Beat.*) And then I see you...you, with all your calmness...your...your acceptance, and your...forgiveness. And I hate you. (*Beat.*) I thought...after all those years...all of those years together that we...and then this happens and it's as if...I never knew you. Not the real one. You live in a completely different world from me. You're somewhere else entirely. It's as if it all...washed over you somehow...as if you're not a part of it. But I can't escape it. It's all around me...all the time. And sometimes it's too much... I... I can't stand it...and I want it all to go away and never think of her again. Just not think of her, as if she'd never existed. If I could just erase her somehow. I know it's wrong, I know I shouldn't, but I can't help it...because it would all be so much easier. I could just be me again. (*Beat.*) But I can't. I can't escape. Every single day that I wake up, every room I walk into, all that I do reminds me of her. Everything here reminds me of her. (*Beat.*) Except you.

EILEEN

(Monologue 1)

Age range: 30s – 60s

From the play *WYWH*, included in the collection *Going Solo: One-Act Plays for One Actor.*

Eileen's young son went missing a number of years ago, and since then she's lived her life as something of a recluse. Despite her warm, kind-hearted demeanor, her inner grief is never too far from the surface. Here she describes the events of that fateful day and its immediate aftermath.

The character as written in the play is in her mid-fifties, but there is nothing in the text here to prevent a younger actor from taking on this monologue.

Billy disappeared 10 years ago – almost to the day. He was 7-years-old and I was peeling potatoes. He came running into the kitchen asking for money for an ice cream. I told him he could take some from the jar on the counter and off he went, down to Mr. Hobson's on the corner, in his little yellow sweater with the hole under the arm that I never did get around to mending. And that was it…he was gone. He never did make it to Mr. Hobson's, according to Mr. Hobson. He just upped and disappeared…as if by magic. (*Beat.*) They searched the neighborhood with a fine-toothed comb, of course. Police, friends, neighbors – they all pitched in. It was all over the news, on the television, in the papers. Billy's face was everywhere…everywhere except back home. Someone had put his photograph on a flyer with a telephone number you could call if you had any information. That flyer was posted everywhere you looked. Every tree, every lamppost – you couldn't miss it. But then, as time went on, his story began to disappear from the news, the searches were finally called off, and the flyers became faded and torn and…blew away in the wind. Everyone moved on…everyone else, that is. (*Beat.*) A couple of years ago, as I was rummaging through an old drawer looking for what I couldn't tell you now, I came upon one of those old flyers. Gave me quite a start, it did. Suddenly there was Billy looking up at me…with that quizzical expression he sometimes had. I felt just like I'd been run through with a sword. I couldn't move. I just froze up, staring back at Billy's face and the four words in big, black print written underneath it that simply said, "Have you seen me?"

LEAH

(Monologue 2)

Age range: 30s – 60s

From the play *Leah's Gals*.

A tragicomedy loosely based on King Lear and set in the American South, Leah's Gals centers on the formidable, scrappy matriarch Leah and her three daughters. Having recently maneuvered herself into a rather vulnerable position, Leah now finds her eldest daughter attempting to cut her down to size, provoking a torrent of fury and venom at such a betrayal. Fair warning: this one's not for the faint of heart.

Written as a woman of more advanced years in the original play, there's nothing in the text of this particular piece to prevent a younger actor from tackling it.

As with the other monologues taken from Leah's Gals, if you find the Southern accent here a little challenging, feel free to iron out any of the colloquial language and phrasings into more formal English.

The only peace I gotta make with myself right now is why I never listened to your daddy when he begged me on his hands an' knees to get you aborted. Probably would o' stuck around a few more months if I had. Offered to pay, too. Lookin' back, seems like I played a losin' hand that day. (*Beat.*) To think I listened to all your lies o' love an' devotion, an' let myself get taken in. All them sweet words spoutin' outta that festerin' sore you call a heart. All that syrup dribblin' from ya mouth was nothin' but pus. By God, whatever Patina's faults, they sure do look small compared to the lyin', thievin', money grubbin' little vulture I see before me now. (*Putting her hands to her face.*) God dammit, Leah! How could ya o' been so god damned stupid? (*Looking skyward.*) Sweet Lord above, if yer up there, let me ask just this one thing o' ya – just one thing – 'fore I come up there an' join ya, an' that's to strike this woman with cancer. Put a tumor in her, Lord, an' let it keep growin' an' growin' inside her, wrackin' her body with pain an' disease 'til she can't hardly stand it no more, an' don't let it take her 'til nine months have passed so she'll know what it was like for me – with her.

LUKA

Age range: 20s – 60s (Cross-castable)

From the play *The End of the World.*

Predominantly set in a bed and breakfast establishment located somewhere in the afterlife, The End of the World finds its protagonist, Valentine, encountering a rather eccentric array of visitors and fellow guests during his stay. Here he is confronted by Luka, a mordant, world-weary soul who upbraids him on the deviousness and complacency of Western democracies.

Luka is described in the play as being of Eastern European decent, so you might find a corresponding accent useful here, though it's by no means necessary and will work perfectly well without one.

People can be dead and living at the same time, no? Don't you know that by now? There are those that are dead inside but still take breath. You see, you hear, you know. Don't pretend you don't. Or what? You don't have television? All your Western advancements don't include the television set? Or maybe you don't like reality TV? Or maybe it's not reality until you find yourself sitting face to face with it at the breakfast table, is that it? Well, who can blame you really, sitting there in your comfortable home, looking at the terrible images and feeling so bad for a few guilt-ridden seconds when reading your newspapers and chewing your toast, only to turn the page to smaller tales of smaller pains that cause you smaller sadness. It's not your fault. You didn't cause it, after all – who can blame you? *(Beat.)* Except me...looking at you – all of the power and asleep at the wheel. Do we intervene or don't we? What will it cost us? Will we be re-elected if we act? It's a human catastrophe. It's abhorrent. We deplore it. We condemn it. We do nothing. Better to wait...wait until the killing is done. Rwanda, Bosnia, Somalia, Kosovo, Aleppo, South Sudan...so many conflicts, so many conflicting opinions, so much talk, and so much death. So they pick and choose their humanitarian gestures with the steely eye of a seasoned gambler. The scales of power are laden with guilt, cleansed by a moral cause, and replenished by a lucrative book deal upon retirement. (*Beat.*) And on it goes...

WOMAN

(Monologue 3)

Age range: 20s – 60s

From the play *The Replica*, included in the collection *Going Solo: One-Act Plays for One Actor.*

An abused wife is the focus of The Replica, and here we find her recalling the early days of her marriage to husband Karl, including the night of his arrest. While her tone may seem genial and nonchalant, there exists a discernable disconnect between her words and her demeanor, almost as if she were talking about someone else's experiences rather than her own.

A proposal of marriage finally brought an end to my roundelay of rejection. For the first few years things went relatively smoothly. Karl didn't want me to work, so I didn't. He made very good money – what was the point? I stopped writing, too, the impetus having abandoned me after the resounding thud of my initial efforts. About all I did do after a while was smile and nod at Karl's side at every party and business dinner he paraded me at. I wanted to get pregnant, but Karl said the timing was wrong for children. It would have been difficult anyway, as we rarely ever made love, and even then Karl always seemed to have trouble reaching orgasm. He told me he had a low libido. I believed him. It made me feel better. (*Beat.*) On the night Karl was arrested I was watching "The Bridge on the River Kwai" on the television. As I sat contemplating Alec Guinness' blind commitment to a construction that could only serve to perpetuate his imprisonment, Karl was being finger-printed and having his picture taken. He'd been caught engaged in a sex act with a young man with a pierced lip in the men's room in one of the larger department stores. Mr. Buchenroth was summoned, conversations took place, smiles were exchanged, hands shaken, and nothing more was heard of it. As I'd reminded myself while sitting in Karl's brand new Porsche 924 just a few weeks earlier, it's amazing what money can buy. When the bridge finally exploded, tumbling down into the river, my sense of catharsis was palpable. (*Beat.*) Ah, the magic of the movies.

LEAH

(Monologue 3)

Age range: 40s – 60s

From the play *Leah's Gals*.

Loosely based on the tragedy of King Lear and set in the American South, the normally dauntless and indefatigable Leah now finds herself at a distinct disadvantage, having been betrayed by her two eldest daughters. Here she's just been rebuffed at the home of her middle daughter, Zarconia, and is about to leave, but not before issuing a few acrimonious words of warning before she does so.

As with the other monologues taken from Leah's Gals, if you find the Southern accent here a little challenging, feel free to iron out any of the colloquial language and phrasings into more formal English.

Yeah…nothin'…I'm nothin'. And don't you worry – I'm goin'. I ain't gonna be messin' up your nice, pretty porch no more. (*Building in intensity and rancor.*) But let me tell ya this before I do. Life might o' disappointed me more times than not, an' you might o' finally broke my heart for good on this here night, an' maybe you ain't got it in ya to look upon me as anythin' more than some used-up, worthless old bag lady right now…some pain in the ass that's gone an' outlived her use. But just you know this…as long as I got blood coursin' through ma veins, I'm gonna find the will to make you an' ya sister curse the day you ever drew breath. I gotta lifetime o' bile all bottled up inside o' me, so you better start prayin' to

Jesus 'cause it's comin' your way, an' ya won't know when an' ya won't know where. But when it does come, just know there ain't gonna be no one sheddin' no tears over your stinkin' carcass, 'cause most folks know yer dead inside already. Why else d'ya think all them babies died in yer belly? (*Beat.*) You got that! (*Bursting with fury.*) *You got that!*

CHRISTINE

(Monologue 3)

Age range: 30s – 50s

From the play *The Treachery of Images.*

When a couple's daughter is raped and murdered, the strain put on their relationship is understandably immense. This is not helped, however, by the divergent paths each has taken in their response to the tragedy. While the child's mother, Christine, is overwhelmed by grief and anger, her husband Tom has adopted a more forgiving, magnanimous attitude toward their recent harrowing experience. Here Christine describes, in a rather detached, objective manner, her initial reaction upon hearing the horrific news and of her subsequent shock and confusion at her husband's surprisingly placid demeanor.

In the original play, Christine is described as a woman of middle age, but in this monologue there's nothing included in the text to prevent the age range from being broadened a little.

When my husband first called me at the school to inform me that our daughter had been murdered – strangled to death – by an up-and-coming serial killer...though I'm not sure if three makes you up-and-coming or having arrived, but three it was...I thought...well, actually, I didn't think anything. My mind just sort of stopped. There was too much to compute, I suppose. Too out of the ordinary. Was it a joke? Was it really him? He would never do something like that as a joke. He would never do something like that, period. And where would be the joke in it? Was I imagining it? Imagining I'm on the phone with my husband, and he's telling me my daughter's dead? A day dream I was having that's suddenly gotten out of hand? Everything stopped. Nothing was real. The room began to move around me. Who was this person on the phone? When would I wake up? (*Beat.*) The...creature...the "person" in question, was, as it turns out, a product of Sierra Leone, who'd slithered his way to Europe, snuck past border enforcement at Calais, and arrived in England with no money, little education, and a very strong pair of hands. He also, we later learned, was in possession of a highly-charged libido that found immense satisfaction in coitus post-mortem...or screwing the dead, if you prefer. All of this, naturally, I found quite disturbing. (*Beat.*) So...when it had sunk in and, uh...well...sunk me...I turned, dependently...needily, even...to my husband, the kindly, all-forgiving career guidance counselor, seeking, I suppose...a little guidance. Somehow I imagined that together we'd find some way of...grappling with it...sharing our grief...our loss...getting through it. (*Beat.*) But...much to my surprise, he wasn't there. It wasn't him. He'd become someone else. Someone I didn't know. Someone who walked around with a beneficent smirk on their face, and who suddenly seemed oblivious to the fact that their very own child had just been raped and brutally murdered...though not necessarily in that order.

EILEEN

(Monologue 2)

Age range: 40s – 60s

From the play *WYWH*, included in the collection *Going Solo: One-Act Plays for One Actor.*

Eileen is a warm-hearted, often jovial woman, but the pain and heartache she experienced over the disappearance of her young son, Billy, some years ago has, understandably, never left her. Here she ponders the fate of her child and tells of the email she recently sent him.

According to studies, the murder of an abducted child is a rare event, and of those that are, 74% are dead within 3 hours of the abduction. So, since no body was ever found, I know that Billy's still out there somewhere. And that's a comfort…some of the time. (*Beat.*) He'd be all grown up now, of course. Maybe even has a little 7-year-old of his own. Who knows? But I know he's there. I can feel it. I can feel his presence sometimes…out there…somewhere. (*Beat.*) I think he just got a bit confused, that's all. Got a bit distracted and confused and wandered off and got lost. And some nice family found him and took him indoors and made him something to eat and took care of him and…and when they found out what a lovely little boy he was they just couldn't bear to part with him. And I can't blame them really, because…because he was ever such a lovely boy. Who could ever bear to part with a lovely little thing like that? It would break your heart. (*Pause.*) I sent him an email yesterday. In the address line I just put "Billy." In the subject line I just wrote…WYWH – Wish You Were Here. A few minutes later it came back to me with a message from someone called "The Postmaster" saying, "Transmission failure. Addressee 'Billy' could not be found." (*With a nod of her head.*) Quite right. (*Looking upward.*) But I still think about you every single day, Billy – every single one of them. And don't ever think I don't, 'cause I do. 'Cause I still miss you just like it was yesterday. Just yesterday. (*Beat.*) WYWH, Billy. (*Beat.*) WYWH. (*Beat.*) Sad face.

LEAH

(Monologue 4)

Age range: 40s – 60s

From the play *Leah's Gals.*

A decidedly longer monologue this one, and just as in the storm on the heath scene in King Lear – the play on which Leah's Gals is loosely based – we find the proud but broken matriarch Leah raging at the heavens amid an onslaught of rain and thunder. But whereas in Lear it is the storm itself that is somehow personified, here Leah is venting all of her fury directly at God, the rain and thunder perceived as yet more misery being heaped upon her by the Almighty.

As with the other monologues taken from Leah's Gals, if you find the Southern accent here a little challenging, feel free to iron out any of the colloquial language and phrasings into more formal English. Also, any profanity can easily be switched out with words less likely to cause offense, should that be deemed necessary or prudent.

(*With a roaring, guttural cry to the heavens.*) *WHAT?* (*Beat.*) What d'ya want from me? What else? What else? (*Beat.*) Yeah, I hear ya, I hear ya – so ya can just shut the fuck up! Yeah, yeah, yeah! Throw it all down! Bring it all on! Do yer worst! Ya think I give a damn? Ya think I care? Shout an' scream an' spit on me all ya want, it ain't gonna change nothin' for me 'cause it's already fucked, so fuck you, ya hear me? Yell! Scream! Bang bang, you're dead! Come on, strike me down, ya lousy coward! C'mon! What ya gonna do? Look at me –

I'm already in the gutter – it's all a god damned gutter. Let it all rain down, burn it all up, there ain't nothin' worth savin' down here. You think you're standin' 'bove me, passin' judgment? Ya think ya can shout at me an' piss on me an' make me feel just about as bad as anyone can, ya two-bit, backstabbin' son of a bitch? Well, yer too late! (*Shaking her fist in the air, becoming ever more delirious.*) *Too late!* I was damned from the minute they dragged me outta o' ma Mama's body! An' they had to drag me, see – *drag me* – 'cause I knew...I knew what a shitty place it was they was draggin' me to, see? An' I hung on, I hung on with ma fingers, clawin' at her insides, 'cause I knew, so I kept clawin' an' fightin', fightin'. Fightin' ever since. An' ya know...ya know...I ain't never stopped. An' I guess when ya weigh it all up, it's all a great big sack o' shit that ain't worth fightin' for nohow. Shit, I ain't scared o' you! Human nature don't answer to no one, neither, see? We're a law unto ourselves down here...an' it ain't pretty. (*Beat.*) Let me tell ya somethin'... let me...let me tell ya somethin'...I remember...I remember ma Daddy...an' I *loved* ma Daddy, I loved ma Daddy more than anyone...an' I remember him touchin' me, see, an' puttin' his fingers where he weren't s'posed to, an' I cried an' I cried, but it was ma Daddy, ya know what I'm sayin? It was ma Daddy, so I cried but I let him do it, 'cause it was human nature, see, but it hurt, but it was ma Daddy, but now yer shoutin' down at me like I did somethin' wrong, an' maybe I did an' maybe I didn't, I'm just sayin' it's all nature – maybe it ain't natural, but it's nature...it's all us doin' what ya made us able to – an' maybe that's what we are. Maybe...maybe yer own flesh an' blood don't mean nothin' 'cause it ain't flesh an' blood, it's just skin an' it ain't no deeper than that – just skin holdin' it all in, coverin' up all the dogs an' jackals inside. Pelts on a bunch o' god damned animals. Is that what we are? 'Cause if that's it. . .if that's all we are underneath it all, then maybe it's. . .maybe we should all just. . .'cause I don't wanna. . .I don't wanna. . .I don't. . . (*Cowering on her haunches.*) Don't. . .don't. . .don't. . .

DRAMATIC MONOLOGUES

Male

TRISTRAM

Age range: 20s – 60s

From the play *Suburban Redux*.

Tristram, a rather shy, awkward young man with a slight stutter, has just been rebuffed by the high-spirited woman he adores. What began as a friendship soon developed into something far more amorous in nature on Tristram's part, but when his confession of love is met with rejection, he attempts – with painful honesty – not only to accept her decision but to justify it. This is a monologue that will certainly speak to anyone who has ever felt less than adequate in the presence of more dazzling, vivacious company.

While the character in the original play is portrayed as a man of younger years, there is nothing here in the text to prevent an actor of any age from performing this monologue.

No, no, it's quite all right. And it isn't self-pity, it-it's self-knowledge. I'm quite aware of who I am. And I'm quite aware that I've never had a-a particularly interesting or revealing thing to say or contribute in my entire life. And you needn't be kind, I-I'm not in need of sympathy. Self-knowledge is a source of strength if one's able to embrace it. But the fact remains, when you get right down to it, I'm a decidedly dull individual, and it was stupid and vain of me to imagine you could regard me as anything else. But it's who I am. I don't wish to be dull. Who would? I can imagine nothing more wonderful than to be an object of fascination in the eyes of another. But no matter how I try it's not to be

– not for me, at least. (*Beat.*) But, you see, unlike your husband, whenever I look in the mirror I'm more than capable of facing the truth – however sobering. (*Beat.*) Oh, don't get me wrong – I-I'm not saying I don't find *life* interesting. I do. I find it immeasurably interesting, as I do people, and art, and music, and literature…and you. I think that must be why I love you a-and love being with you as much as I do – you fill in the bits of me that are missing. When I'm with you I feel as though I *am* interesting and witty and clever. And I'm sure any number of psychologists would be happy to tell me that that's vicarious a-and weak and wrong of me, but you see…it makes me so very happy. (*Beat.*) But with you, as with the arts, I'm simply a receptacle for someone else's abilities. I absorb them, I feed on them, they enrich me, but at the end of the day…I bring nothing to the table.

MALCOLM

Age range: 20s – 50s

From the play *A Small Act of Vandalism*, included in the collection *Going Solo: One-Act Plays for One Actor.*

Malcolm, a gentle soul with a troubled mind, is haunted by the last request his sick and dying mother made of him – that he end her suffering and allow her to die with a little dignity. There was no one in the world he loved more – he loved her more than life itself – but now he must live with the knowledge that he took that life.

Though a difficult and painful subject, the tone here should not be unduly maudlin. Though clearly tortured by his actions that day, Malcolm is still able to view the overall situation with a certain degree of pragmatism.

Mother was very ill, you see. Very ill indeed. She had…well, something I neither remember nor found pronounceable to begin with. But whatever it was, it was causing her system to atrophy. It was neurological, that much I can tell you. And progressive. And eventually, without aid…without artificial assistance…her body was going to forget how to breathe. And she knew it, and I knew it. They'd told us. But…while she still could…while she still had the chance to make a choice…she asked me to stop it. Stop it all. (*Beat.*) It was my mother. She was facing the unthinkable. And so…I agreed. I loved her, you see. I'd have done anything for her. And I did. (*Pause.*) It was a simple plan. I was to take one of her favorite cushions – one she'd embroidered herself as a girl, when her head was full of thoughts of what lay ahead – and I was to hold it gently against her weakened face until what little life left in her was extinguished. (*Beat.*) And I was a good son. I did what she asked. What she needed...so desperately. And I made her feel better. And I'm glad of that. I try to focus on that. But I'm not always very successful at it, to tell you the truth. (*Beat.*) Because now she's gone...and resting in peace. Hopefully. But me...I'm still here. And however you want to look at it and no matter how you word it...I killed my mother. I killed her. And I love her so much, and I'm so angry at her. So angry, you wouldn't believe. But it's not her fault. She's not to blame. And neither am I...but I'm still angry. Because I hate life now. I can hardly live with myself. (*Beat.*) I'm hardly living.

TOM

(Monologue 1)

Age range: 20s – 60s

From the play *The Treachery of Images*.

The murder of their young daughter has understandably taken a heavy toll on the marriage of Tom and Christine, and Tom's surprising public statements and his general air of calm acceptance of the situation has now led Christine to question the authenticity of his grief. Here Tom attempts to set the record straight over what his daughter meant to him and to defend his somewhat controversial stance.

Tom is level-headed and rational, sometimes to the point of appearing impassive, though less so in this particular monologue. In the original play he's also a man of middle age, but since the age of the daughter is not indicated here, the age range can be extended.

You know damned well that I...that I loved that girl more than anything else in this world. Even more than you. (*Beat.*) You know I did. (*Beat.*) There was nothing I was more proud of than to have been a...a part of bringing her into this world. That...wonderful, beautiful person that she was. I suppose in some ways she...she validated me. To have created something so...bright and full of life and hope amidst all the...well, all the rest of it. I suppose it made me feel that perhaps that was some kind of reason for it after all...or a reason for me, at any rate. Because when you take a good, hard look at it all, it really doesn't amount to a whole lot. Not really. A job, a career...what does it all mean when all's said and done? What do you leave behind that couldn't have been done by someone else? But her...she was uniquely mine and she did matter. She did mean something. And I don't have to justify myself or my reasoning to anybody. I don't care what they say or what they think. (*Beat.*) They'll do it anyway.

DENNY

(Monologue 1)

Age range: 20s – 60s

From the play *One Night Only*, included in the collection *Going Solo: One-Act Plays for One Actor.*

Denny is a prison inmate on death row in a Southern U.S. penitentiary. On the last night of his life he decides to conduct an interview with himself while awaiting the imminent arrival of his executioner, who is in an adjoining room and visible through a semitransparent window. Here we find him recalling his initial motivation for contemplating the act of murder as well as his moral justification for choosing to act on those thoughts.

While a Southern American accent might seem obligatory here, it most definitely isn't. There are almost 3,000 inmates on death row in the United States (at the time of writing) hailing from all parts of the country, as well as roughly 35 foreign nationals from across the globe.

You wanna know about the first time? (*Beat.*) The first time, the first time, yes, yes, yes...well, well, well...the first time, yes, well, I'd been thinking about it, you see – about killing someone – for quite some time. Quite some time. Years, as a matter of fact. And then one day I just decided to do it, just because I could, and...because I wanted to know what it felt like, and because I had the ability and the intellectual curiosity, and because...well, I think it's fairly safe to assume I was probably having a *bad day*. (*Beat.*) And they said, "But you knew it was wrong, Denny." (*Beat.*) But wrong? What's wrong? It's only wrong if you choose to call it wrong. Same as right. Someone decides what's called wrong and what's called right. They just give it a name. They say that that's wrong and that's right, that's yours and that's mine. Doesn't mean they're right. It's just a choice. Look at him in there – he's about to kill me, and what's more he's being paid to do it by the same people who say what I did was wrong. So you tell me? And no one paid me. And I wouldn't say he looks particularly bothered about it either, would you? Look at him, shuffling around in there like he had all day. (*Beat.*) Hey! (*Beat.*) *Hey!* (*Beat, then with ferocity.*) *HEY! I DON'T HAVE ALL DAY!*

Dramatic Male

CUTHBERT

Age range: 20s – 30s

From the play *Suburban Redux*.

The play Suburban Redux is akin to a modern day comedy of manners. At this point in the proceedings, however, it's all drama as Cuthbert brings home his girlfriend, Trixie, to finally meet his capricious mother and her gentleman friend. Ill-disposed to any woman who might cramp her son's lifestyle, his mother's welcoming of Trixie is far from gracious, and here Cuthbert's patience has finally snapped as he calls her to account in no uncertain terms.

You want an explanation? All right, I'll give it to you. He's a dunderhead and you're a hypocrite! And if you want to know how I dare speak to you like that, it's simple – I just open my mouth and out it pops. It doesn't take daring to speak the truth, just a little outrage. And I'm sick of it! You've done nothing but take snide pot shots at Trixie from the outset. Clearly you were predisposed to dislike her – no matter what her qualities – before you even stepped through that door. It has nothing to do with being misconstrued; it's a matter of saying one thing and meaning another – a talent at which you remain unrivalled. It's that smiling, highly glossed lip service you pay your way through this world with. (*Beat.*) It's a façade, Mother, all of it. Just as when you told me – in front of witnesses – that you'd found it within yourself to accept me for who I was. But when it comes right down to it – to dealing with the flesh and blood reality of it – it's a different matter, and the façade crumbles and all that's left is the hollow gesture it was attempting to mask.

DAD

(Monologue 1)

Age range: Late 30s – 60s

From the play *Dedication*, included in the collection *The War Plays: Four One-Acts*.

The father of a young soldier killed in battle is the subject in question in this particular monologue. A practical-minded man, he carries an air of disillusionment about him and has difficulty expressing his emotions. Here he's just arrived at the gravesite of his son which he hasn't visited in quite some time. As he stands before the headstone he attempts to explain his long absence.

Hello son. (*Beat.*) Not sure what I'm supposed to...well, to say in this kind of a...situation. Never was very religious, as you know. So I'm not really sure how this works. So if I miss something out...you know...sorry about that. Guess I'll just start off with the basics. So...well...hello son. (*Beat.*) I, um...I meant to come by before. Long before. But...well, you know how it is...what with your mom falling apart like she has – completely understandable, though, and I'm not complaining, but...well, it does make it harder – and work's been piling on the overtime like no one's business, and sometimes I hardly seem to get a minute to think. So what with one thing and another, it's been really hard to find the time to come by. (*Beat.*) And I suppose...I suppose if I was being honest, I've been...well, I've been putting it off a bit, too. Been thinking about you quite a bit, see, son. Quite a bit.

But not here. I don't like to think of you here. I think about you how it used to be...such a short time ago. Seems like forever now. But coming here...it makes it real. Makes me face it. And the truth is I haven't been doing all that well with this myself. Have to try, see, 'cause of your mom. But that's why you haven't seen me. Been avoiding it, I guess. But...well, here I am...and there it is...the plain truth – carved in stone.

JACK

(Monologue 1)

Age range: 20s – 50s

From the play *The One-Eyed Guru.*

Jack, a plain-spoken pragmatist with a cynical edge, has been waiting up for his wife, Rachel, who failed to arrive home at her usual time. When she finally does show up, however, she regales him with a bizarre tale of her exploits that day which culminates in her presenting him with irrefutable proof of his infidelity. Here Jack comes clean about his duplicity, but not without making a spirited attempt at justifying it.

Not that you care or I care but she really wasn't anything. Nothing at all. Just a cheap lay. She came off as the type that wanted it bad enough that once they'd had it you'd think that would be it. But not her. A couple of drinks and a sit-down pizza and you'd think I'd proposed. Started getting pushy. I couldn't get rid of her. Started wanting more and more. Started making threats. I ignored it in the beginning. Who wouldn't – some brainless tart going through the motions? Then she starts ringing here. Nothing to say…just wanted to "talk." That's when I knew. I knew it was just a matter of time. (*Beat.*) But remorse? You've got some nerve you have, after I've sat up here half the night, not knowing if you were alive or dead. Not knowing where the hell you were as you waltz in here and start spinning me some crackpot tale about some old pervert and my mother's cancer. Why the hell would I be feeling anything that resembles remorse? Pity is more like it. *(Beat.)* But you see, that's half your problem – you don't know when to stop. You never did. You never let anything go. You always have to stretch it out into some never ending soap opera. *(Beat.)* It was too much, Rachel. *You're* too much. You suffocate. I'm only human, for God's sake. I only did what anyone else would've done – I needed some breathing space, that's all. I needed an outlet...for my head. And tonight's the best example of all. Any normal person would've walked in here and said, "Jack, I know you're having an affair with Melanie – what are we going to do about it?" But not you. You've got no time for logic or common sense. You have to spend hours stitching together some ludicrous, psychopathic story whose sole purpose is to mess with my head. Is it any wonder...I mean, really, is it?

FRANKIE

Age range: 20s – 30s

From the play *Leah's Gals*.

In the play Leah's Gals, a tragicomedy loosely based on King Lear, the indomitable matriarch Leah has asked her three daughters for declarations of undying love. When her youngest daughter, Patina, refuses to do so, she is disowned by her mother, forfeiting a substantial financial endowment in the process. Fearing that her actions may have alienated her boyfriend, Frankie, she braces herself for rejection. But the spirited, good-natured and upstanding Frankie soon sets her straight on the true nature of his intentions.

If you find the Southern accent here a little challenging, feel free to iron out any of the colloquial language and phrasings into more formal English.

God dammit, Patty, ya had next to nothin' when I met ya, ya had next to nothin' this mornin' when I got up, an' ya still have next to nothin' now. What in the name o' the Lord or Satan makes you think that I'm gonna have different feelin's for ya now than I did a day ago? Or six months ago? Who d'ya think I am? Is that how you see me – as some kinda speculator, waitin' to see how much ma stocks worth 'fore decidin' whether to trade? (*Beat.*) You got me wrong, Patty. You got me all wrong. See, when I saw your sisters over there today, carryin' on like they was in a soap opera, gushin' an' fawnin' all over yer mama like that, well I gotta confess it fair made me sick to ma stomach. It was like watchin' a couple o' dogs on their hind legs, with yer mama danglin' a bone at em. But you…you were just you. Beautiful you, not takin' no bait, not takin' no bull, just tellin' the God's honest truth. An' dammit, I couldn't o' felt more proud. An' as for bein' rich, hell Patty, the day I met you I was like a prospector hittin' gold. A man don't get much richer than I am right now. I swear I feel like I'm livin' a dream with you, an' if you don't hurry up an' make an honest man outta me I'm gonna go clear outta ma mind!

TOM

(Monologue 2)

Age range: 20s – 60s

From the play *The Treachery of Images*.

Tom is very discerning and reasoned in his approach to life, always seeking elucidation of its ambiguities. Here we find him attempting to explain to his understandably outraged wife, Christine, his motivation for visiting the killer of their young daughter at the prison in which he's housed.

Though a man of middle age in the source play, nothing in the text here prevents this monologue from being performed by an actor of any age.

I'll tell you why I went there. I went there to…to try to make some sense out of the nonsensical. To get some kind of… meaning…where none existed. (*Beat.*) I'm a pretty logical person by nature. You know this. You don't always like it, but it's the way I am. I'm also aware that…some things happen in life that don't make a whole lot of sense, no matter how much you wish they did. A cable snaps, a computer malfunctions, a car skids…all sorts of little ways for great tragedies to be wrought that don't give us the comfort of reason. They just happen. A life is lost and shockwaves reverberate around those left behind until the end, all wondering why? Why them? Why their daughter? Their son? Mother? (*Beat.*) But I'm not good with random, with chance, with all that being in the wrong place at the wrong time stuff.

Some people are. Some people can chalk it up to some sort of existential, incomprehensible mad bit of bad luck in a grand scheme they know nothing of, however great their pain. Some find solace in placing the responsibility in the lap of God, his reasoning being mysterious but absolute. But none of that works for me. (*Beat.*) I needed some form of accounting, even if the facts – the horror of the facts – told me there could be none.

DENNY

(Monologue 2)

Age range: 20s – 60s

From the play *One Night Only*, included in the collection *Going Solo: One-Act Plays for One Actor*.

This is the last night of Denny's life. A prison inmate on death row in a Southern U.S. penitentiary, Denny's moment of reckoning has finally arrived. In his last remaining moments he's decided to conduct an interview with himself, perhaps to distract his mind from what is about to take place. Here he describes the exhilaration he would experience while in the act of taking the life of another.

As mentioned before, though a Southern American accent might appear to be required here, it certainly is not. With close to 3,000 inmates on death row in the United States (at the time of writing) hailing from all parts of the country, as well as roughly 35 foreign nationals from across the globe, any accent would suffice here.

You wanna know what it felt like…that first time? (*Beat.*) Oh, that's…that's hard to answer…hard to describe. There aren't words, you see? It's like…it's like the biggest rush you could ever imagine. Forget drugs and sex, this was…this was off the goddamn charts. In that moment, you're…you're everything. You're…you're God. There's this face, see…and it's disfigured with terror…and it's staring up at you, knowing its very existence, its very being, is in your hands…the same hands around its neck squeezing the life out of it. And you're

God. And it knows it. (*Beat.*) But then…near the end, the face changes. The look of terror turns to awe…*awe*. I am the power. I am God. They see it. And finally, right before they slip away…the best part of all – and this was the same with all the girls, from the first to the last, the pretty and the ugly – they all looked the same at the very last moment. Just the same. Just before they slipped away there'd be this look of total innocence in their faces…like children…innocent little children…even the old ones. They'd look up at me with such…such innocence…like a child to a parent…not knowing what was happening to them or where they were going. Not knowing anything. (*Beat.*) And then they were gone…released…cleansed…at peace. I'd given them back their innocence, you see?

DAD

(Monologue 2)

Age range: Late 30s – 60s

From the play *Dedication*, included in the collection *The War Plays: Four One-Acts.*

In Dedication, the father of a young soldier lost in combat visits his son's gravesite, where he proceeds to engage in a conversation with him. In the play, the son actually appears on stage, standing behind his father, though they never actually look at each other throughout their exchange. In this moment, the father is sharing the perspective of the conflict from those back home and the ever-changing justifications given for its advent.

Yep, son...I was taken for a fool. (*Beat.*) First off they were jabberin' on about "weapons of mass destruction" – like they'd never existed before...like killin' a whole bunch of people with a weapon was somethin' new. But the phrase was new and it sounded good. Spooked us out at the time anyhow. So off you were packed to play their games, while we stayed behind, worryin' and stickin' magnets on our cars and pretendin' it was World War Two all over again. (*Beat.*) Only problem was...there weren't any. So then they harped on about what a great thing it was we were doin' by toppling this bastard dictator who'd killed and tortured his own people – guess they must've picked his name out of a hat. And so on you fought...or sat...or patrolled...all the time gettin' picked off...one by one. (*Beat.*) They said we'd be welcomed as heroes and liberators, just like back in France in '44. But they were wrong again. They played up a few scenes for the cameras and tried to convince us, but the truth of it was soon made clear enough. They just saw us for what we were – invaders. And all our big bombs and fancy technology didn't mean a damn, 'cause they went ahead and did what every other land in history's done when they've been invaded by foreigners…they turned on us. (*Beat.*) And then…then the story changed again and all we heard about was how they were turnin' on each other – that the whole place would go up in flames if we weren't there to keep a lid on it. A mess we'd made, but there you go – you reap what you sow. And all the news was of Arab against Arab and tribe against tribe, religion against religion, or whatever the hell their history of problems was that were now supposed to be our problems…my problems…your problems. (*Beat.*) And that's when we lost you.

MR. JONES

Age range: 20s – 60s

From the play *The Joneses,* included in the collection *The War Plays: Four One-Acts.*

The Joneses is a satire of a real life couple with a very "special relationship." In the play, a married couple have adopted a couple of young boys from the Middle East but soon discover they've bitten off far more than they can chew. The children in question are out of control, filled with bloodlust, and fight each other viciously and constantly. Here we find Mr. Jones, an intransigent, zealous man, steadfastly rejoicing in his decision to adopt, even as his home burns down around him.

Oh thank you, Lord! Thank you for this unshakeable will you've given us. Thank you for bestowing upon us the strength and determination to stand firm in the face of the incredulous. Your words have been my weapons. I am yours, your humble servant, your vessel, your instrument of change. My children are now your children, freed from the grasp of the wailing pagans, free to embrace their new life. And we'll help them; we'll teach them and tame them. Oh, how happy they'll be! Educated and integrated, anglicized and circumcised. They'll dance and sing and praise the day the heavens opened up and changed their world forever. Oh, what model children they'll be, such model children. An example to the world! And they will call me father, and they will take my name, and they will be my legacy when I am gone, these children of the sand. Oh thank you, dear Lord, for leading me on this path, for bringing me to this place. I feel you here. I feel the warmth of your breath, the fire of your passion, the red hot glow of your unending embrace. (*Beat.*) I am with you now, here where I belong. I've come home...home to you. (*Beat.*) You knew I'd come. And I knew you'd be waiting...waiting here for me. (*Beat.*) Waiting with your baptismal fires, your eternal flames. Waiting in that light that never goes out...never goes out.

JACK

(Monologue 2)

Age range: 20s – 50s

From the play *The One-Eyed Guru.*

Jack's wife, Rachel, arrives home very late one evening with a tale of a day spent in the company of a quixotic stranger with paranormal abilities. Jack, however, is a cynic to his core, and in his typically blunt, unvarnished manner he attempts to debunk her story and enlighten her as to the true nature of the world in which she lives.

So tell me, what sage old nuggets of insight did he dole out to you, this tea-swilling witch doctor of yours? Did he tell you that you'd experienced a time of great pain in your life, that someone in your family was ill, and that you had a natural affinity for the color blue? Or was he more specific? Perhaps he revealed to you how the fates had deliberately kiboshed your attempts to buy that jacket in that store in the certain knowledge that one day you'd discover another jacket in another chain store that was going to enrich your life beyond all human comprehension? Or perhaps he dug a little deeper and exposed to you the startling truth of your hidden inner core of complete and utter gullibility? Now, if he'd shown you that I really would be impressed. (*Beat.*) Honestly, I don't know what to tell you. I mean, what you say is all very commendable, but…well, Christ, love, you're about two generations out of sync with the times. You've got your heart in the right place but you've got your head stuck up your ass.

The fact is life's not nice. Nice if it was, but it's not. It's vicious and it's two faced. It's all self-service these days. They've all got dirt under their fingernails, all of them. They're all grubbing around for one thing or another. Whatever you'd like it to be, the truth is you can't trust anyone and nothing is what seems. And unless you wise up to that, you're going to find yourself on the endangered species list – along with the pandas and the whales and the spotted toads.

MAN

Age range: 20s – 60s

From the play *Degraded*, included in the collection *The War Plays: Four One-Acts*.

In the play Degraded we find Amarah, a battered wife ground down by years of abuse and oppression, being visited by a man from the Department of Social Services. It soon becomes apparent, however, that this man is a far cry from the benevolent official he would have her believe. Here her sly, manipulative visitor reveals how he was able to exploit a family tragedy to his own advantage.

I'll let you in on a little secret, shall I? But you mustn't tell anyone. This is just between us. Strictly off the record – our little secret. (*Beat.*) You see, before the death of my brother I'd...I'd started to lose favor at the Department. They'd begun to doubt my abilities and my commitment to the job. They'd even begun to question whether they'd made a mistake in appointing me in the first place. I hate to admit it now, Amarah, but the truth is I'd started to become a little panicked. I felt embarrassed and...yes, even paranoid. You see, one of the principal reasons for my being hired in the first place was due to the long and very close relationship my family had established over the years with many prominent figures within the Department. And I couldn't let them down – I couldn't. The family name was at stake. But still I...I floundered. (*Beat.*) Then my brother was shot. Everything changed. It was profound – quite profound. But while everyone else was grieving and remembering, I...I was quietly

133

smiling. Does that sound bad? But it's true. I smiled. I smiled because I knew – through this unimaginable tragedy – that I'd found the way forward. And I seized upon it. I ran with it, Amarah. I ran and I ran, and I'm still running…but not away – *to*.

TOM

(Monologue 3)

Age range: 20s – 60s

From the play *The Treachery of Images.*

In the days and weeks following the murder of his young daughter, Tom has appeared unusually calm and detached, provoking anger and exasperation from his grief-stricken wife. Here, however, after a particularly virulent confrontation, he finally opens up and reveals to her the reason for his frequently impassive demeanor.

As mentioned previously, though a man of middle age in the source play, nothing in the text here prevents this monologue from being performed by an actor of any age.

I'm…sure that you already know this, but…when the human body is…injured in some way, some quite painful way…it releases endorphins into its system in order to numb itself to that which…might otherwise be unbearable. It creates its own opiate to drug itself into tolerating the intolerable. It's how it survives…or tries to. (*Pause.*) When the police first arrived at my office to…to inform me, consolingly but also quite…bluntly, of what had happened to Susan, I…well, I don't know how to describe it, quite honestly. Initially I…I didn't believe them, it just didn't seem…possible. I thought there must have been some sort of mistake. I told them as much. (*Beat.*) They…assured me that there was no mistake…that identification had been found on her body and...that they were...well, very sorry. (*Beat.*) After they left, I...it didn't so much sink in as...envelop me. Entirely. I wanted to scream. Every part of my body wanted to scream. I thought I would explode. It was too much to take in, to contain. I wanted to scream so loudly that the sheer force of my voice would...make it not true. That I could stop it. (*Beat.*) But I couldn't. I couldn't stop it. And I couldn't scream. (*Beat.*) Instead, this...strange feeling swept over me. Over my mind. Over everything. It was almost physical. I felt it hit me, roll right over me. It hit so hard I thought I would faint. It was like being drunk. Too drunk. Everything was in slow motion, and I was falling... (*Beat.*) And then I was numb. And I think I knew why...in a way. But it didn't matter, because I couldn't control it. It all just sort of shut down...because it had to. But it was okay, you see, because it made it...because...I could breathe again. It suddenly all looked different. It was apart from me. (*Placing his fist against his chest.*) It wasn't in here anymore. It was somewhere else. And so was I. (*Beat.*) And there I've been ever since...hiding...scared...in this...strange calm. Scared but protected...from all that would consume me...submerge me. I'm on an island, you see? And it's very small...and it's very lonely. (*Beat.*) And I can't get off it. Not yet. (*His voice cracking with emotion.*) And this is how I survive. And I know it may seem cowardly...but it's what I must do. I know there are storms and raging seas all around me, but...but here...here on my island, if I look up at the sky...it's blue and it's calm...and it's safe. And if I just keep looking up...then the rest of it...I can let go of. (*Pause.*) Please forgive me.

HORATIO

Age range: 20s – 50s

From the play *The Most Interesting Man in the Whole Wide World*.

Horatio Higgins is a mercurial loner who suffers from delusional disorder. Despite this, however, he has been able to live a relatively high-functioning life. When we meet him here, though, he has reached a point of mental decline that has become perilously unpredictable. During an evening at home with his girlfriend – a sweet, somewhat overweight young woman – he finds himself becoming overwhelmed by the darker forces at play in his mind.

I was just mentioning how beautiful your eyes look this evening. So...so innocent, so...open. It's quite startling. Those two exquisitely defined oval jewels trapped inside that hideous, bloated carcass. It's quite jolting. Such an odd juxtaposition. One can only assume that Mother Nature, when she pieced you together, was either temporarily deranged or is far more vicious than she would have us believe. But what's to be done? We are not the creators. We are simply products, each and every one of us. The most we can ever hope to do, in our own humble way, in our little corner of the world, is to clean up a few of the mistakes – errors of judgment. We all make them – even Mother Nature. Those things that came to be that in an ideal world shouldn't have – however well intended. Like a master sculptor intolerant of a flawed bust – so he busts it. Smashes it...cleans the slate. You weren't meant to be. You were something that lived that shouldn't have. Like a baby with spina bifida. It's painful. It's heartbreaking. Shouldn't have been – plain for anyone to see. Better off not being. You're as nice and inoffensive as they come, but what's the point to you? You take up too much room. You're too large, dull and all-consuming to validate your being here. You take up too much space – you eat too much. There are literally thousands – hundreds of thousands – of tiny little children dying every day from hunger, malnutrition, disease, unexploded ordinance, land mines, land grabs…and then there's you. All those tiny little innocent children, full of potential, full of promise, snuffed out every second of the day, and yet…there you are – big, huge, hard to satiate you. Pleasant enough when she's sober, annoying as fuck when she's drunk, *you*. (*Beat*.) So you tell me…where's the justice?

DENNY

(Monologue 3)

Age range: 20s – 60s

From the play *One Night Only*, included in the collection *Going Solo: One-Act Plays for One Actor*.

These are the final moments of Denny's life as he awaits execution on death row in a Southern U.S. penitentiary. Occupying his time by conducting an interview with himself, in his final question he asks if he feels any remorse for his actions.

As previously mentioned, if it appears a Southern American accent might appear necessary here, it isn't. With close to 3,000 inmates on death row in the United States (at the time of writing) hailing from all parts of the country, as well as roughly 35 foreign nationals from across the globe, any accent used would be credible.

Fair warning: this particular monologue contains a copious amount of profane language. This is a prison inmate – a serial killer at that – who is moments away from being executed, so his use of profanity would seem almost de rigueur under the circumstances. However, if this would be inappropriate for your audition, as well it may, then simply describe the frontal lobes as being "messed" up, and remove the other instances altogether and it'll work just fine without them.

Remorse? Serial killers can't feel remorse, you should know that? Someone hasn't done their homework very well, have they? Well, it's really quite simple. It's not that we don't...not that I'd want to…we just can't. Something to do with our frontal lobes, see? Read it somewhere. They're all fucked up. Can't feel it. Oh well… (*Pause.*) That said…there was one…one I regretted. The pregnant one. (*Beat.*) How was I to know? I don't have x-ray eyes. And that lying bitch didn't tell me. She didn't show. I didn't know. She should've told me! (*Beat.*) It was in the paper. Not good. You don't hurt kids. Not their fault. Nothing's their fault. They're just innocent…innocent little faces…'til someone takes it away…hurt's em…does stuff. (*Beat.*) No…ya don't hurt kids. (*Beat, then with ever increasing vehemence.*) But…when you're all grown up…well, you gotta take what's coming to ya, just like me, here and now, no fear, not me, don't feel nothin, nothin there, never was, never will be, just me, just me lookin at you, lookin at me, and I swear to God, if you don't quit jerkin me around and get out here now and get this over with, I'm gonna rip these fuckin straps off and come in there and make you wish you'd never been born! I'll rip that fuckin head off your neck and shove it through that fuckin window! I'll squeeze your fuckin eyeballs from their sockets and grind em into this goddamned floor with my bare fuckin feet, so help me God, I will! So help me God, I will! Now for Christ's sake, JUST FUCKIN DO IT!

SERIOCOMIC MONOLOGUES

Female

JOY

Age range: 20s – 50s

From the play *Kitchen Sink Drama*.

Direct and detached to an almost forbidding degree, Joy nevertheless has her heart in the right place. Here she attempts to counsel her sister – in her own inimitable way – who has just confessed to a sexual indiscretion with a complete stranger.

Though there is a suggestion in the monologue that Joy's sister is of a certain age, no such implication is in evidence of Joy's age, so a younger actor could certainly tackle this one. Also, in view of Joy's rather garrulous nature, an increasingly rapid-fire delivery would probably serve this monologue well.

Look, let me just say right now that I am not about to lecture you about things that you, as an informed adult, should already be patently aware of – i.e. that in this day and age you simply cannot go around having unprotected sex with anyone, anywhere, whenever you feel like it. Not just because of the risk of HIV infection, which is, of course, by far the most serious, but for a whole host of other unsavory social calling cards, such as hepatitis, gonorrhea, herpes and crabs, to name but a few; but also because, even at your age, Elaine, you cannot rule out the possibility of pregnancy, because I remember reading some story recently where this French woman conceived at the age of 97, or something hideous like that, and even though it was all done with test tubes and lasers and things, the fact is you're not 97 and stranger things have happened. But more to the point, I desperately hope that you're not one of those troglodytes that still likes to believe that HIV and AIDS are the sole realm of homosexuals and sub-Saharan Africans, because if you are, you're not only an idiot, you're one of those lamentable and all-too-common bi-products of the so-called information age that only ever reads the "informative headline," never the full story. So...rather than lecture you, I will simply say this: what are you doing about it?

MRS. PENNINGTON-SOUTH

(Monologue 1)

Age range: Late 30s – 50s

From the play *Suburban Redux.*

Having raised her son, Cuthbert, in the hope that he was homosexual, the indomitable Mrs. Pennington-South recently had those hopes dashed when Cuthbert came out and confessed his true heterosexuality. Though accepting of him, she nevertheless harbors serious concerns over what this will mean for his future, as she explains here to her young friend, Tristram.

It's worth keeping in mind that although the language here may appear somewhat heightened, this is a matter of crucial importance to Mrs. Pennington-South and she speaks of it with utmost sincerity.

I said what he needed to hear, Tristram. I'm his mother – how could I do less? But saying something and reconciling oneself to it don't always go hand in hand. Of course I want him to be happy. I've made it my personal cause célèbre to ensure that he might find the kind of happiness in life that I could not. And if he feels that pursuing this heterosexual lifestyle of his will somehow bring him that happiness then I must, regardless of my misgivings, allow him that freedom. But the fact remains… (*Beat. Pacing the room.*) The fact remains, Tristram, it's unbearably difficult and painful to have to stand by and watch one's own flesh and blood be swallowed up by this…this tepid, pre-assembled existence that chokes the life out of everything in its path. A place where textured walls are deemed imaginative; a place of endless, humourless dinner parties built around recipes clipped from Woman's Realm. A world of middle ground, middlebrow eyes peeking through net curtains, terrified their hydrangeas – like their personalities – won't be blooming again this year. It's a vortex, Tristram. A huge black hole – with just a hint of beige – perched on the outskirts of life, surrounded by manicured hedgerows, sucking us all in as we blindly lunge at something – anything – to cling to. (*Beat.*) I clung to my son, hoping to save him at least, if not myself. But I see now that it was all in vain – he'd already fallen.

PEGGY

Age range: 20s – 50s

From the play *Big Girl*, included in the collection *Going Solo: One-Act Plays for One Actor*.

Equipped with a sharp mind and an even sharper tongue, Peggy brings her mordant wit to this piece as she discusses the demise of a not so beloved aunt. In the original play she is portrayed as a younger woman, but with no age-related information included in this particular monologue the age range can be broadened. And while Peggy is described as considerably overweight in the play, the extent of her weight issue is referred to in more general terms here, making size a less decisive factor in selecting this monologue for performance. Also, it goes without saying that if you're on the left side of the Atlantic Ocean, you can replace "Mum" with "Mom."

I've always been big. I was born big. I was a big baby. Still am in some respects. In fact, one of the earliest memories I have is of my Aunt Nester staring down at me, her thin lips contorted into a forced expression of adoration, saying to my mother, "My word, you've got a big girl there, haven't you, Georgie." (*Beat.*) She's dead now. Not my mother – my Aunt Nester. A severe stroke whilst pruning her beloved roses in her front garden. She fell into them face first, the thorns of her pride and joy gashing open her wizened face in her moment of need. They did a good job, though – at the mortuary, that is. She looked quite regal, all dished up and served before us, there in her casket. I stared hard at her face but I couldn't see even the trace of a scar. Mum fell apart.

147

Sadly, all I felt was a slight twinge of guilt as I contorted my not-so-thin lips into a forced expression of loss.

MRS. PENNINGTON-SOUTH

(Monologue 2)

Age range: Late 30s – 50s

From the play *Suburban Redux*.

A flamboyant free-spirit, Mrs. Pennington-South's more histrionic tendencies are well-represented in this monologue as she discusses the birth of her son and her nascent fear of abandonment now that he's reached adulthood.

As mentioned previously, despite her propensity for the dramatic, this shouldn't diminish the strength of conviction behind her words in performance.

Do I regret bringing him into the world? Never! No, never! Whatever disappointments I've had in life, he will never be one of them. (*Beat.*) Though I will admit – between you and I – when I first gave birth to him I did, for a moment, think that I'd made the most frightful mistake. I'd wanted him, naturally, but until that day I can honestly say I had no idea that a baby could be so profoundly ugly. Even seasoned members of the maternity staff were shaken by the sight of him. I can still recall the screams from some of the younger nurses. At first they were reluctant to show him to me, fearing I might lapse into some sort of hysteria. But, you know, when I finally did lay eyes upon that strange, marsupial-like thing that had somehow tunneled its way out from inside me, I...I didn't scream – I cried. I cried with joy for the gift of a new life – his and mine. By his birth I felt that I'd been given another chance, too. I'd been given the task of looking after a life – a real human life – and I was determined I'd make it a full one. (*Beat.*) Now I see I was simply deluding myself with such thoughts, and I shall be left behind as he wanders off to make his own little nest in this petrified forest.

MOTHER

Age range: 40s – 60s

From the play *A Rebel Among the Wretched*, included in the collection *The Meta Plays*.

In A Rebel Among the Wretched, it is the voices of the characters themselves that we are hearing, rather than their scripted lines that the actors of the play deliver during performance. The play in question is a critically acclaimed dysfunctional family drama, but despite its success, the character of the matriarch has had enough and wants out. When her 'local boy made good' son shows up and implores her to change her mind, the irascible old woman has a few choice words for both him and his sister.

If you find the Southern accent here a little challenging, feel free to iron out any of the colloquial language and phrasings into more formal English.

Who the hell are you to tell me what I can and can't do? Ya come waltzin' in here after all these years in ya fancy clothes, with ya fancy manners, thinkin you're somethin better than the rest of us. Well, ya ain't! Ya trash. Ya always were an' ya always will be. Trash in a fancy suit's still trash, an' I'm done with the lot o' ya! All them years ago, when ya Pa just up an' left me, right after he'd seeded me with a couple o' brain-dead tit-suckers that made my life feel so much worse than it already was…well, I just plain hated him. I wanted him to die. But I realize now that he was right. Despite all the pain an' bitterness he caused me over the years, I can see now that he

151

did what he had to. He was right to get out – to leave while he still could. He could tell what a big slab o' misery we were dumpin on the world, an' he wanted nothin more to do with it. And now – slow on the uptake as I am – neither do I. The minute I walk off this stage, this whole sad, sorry excuse for a play ceases to be. Without me…ya got nothin.

MRS. PENNINGTON-SOUTH

(Monologue 3)

Age range: Late 30s – 50s

From the play *Suburban Redux*.

Mrs. Pennington-South's natural vivacity and exuberance are curtailed somewhat here, as she is forced to defend her recent behavior to her son, Cuthbert. Raising him in the hope that he was homosexual, her aspirations were recently dashed by his confession of his heterosexuality. Despite her attempts at acceptance and approval, things haven't gone smoothly between them of late and here she endeavors to explain why.

And again, though her words and mannerisms may seem affected, the strength of feeling behind them is very real.

Now just you listen to me, young man. Perhaps I haven't extended all the courtesies one would hope for this afternoon, and perhaps I haven't been as gracious as I might, and if that is so, then I apologise. But you seem to forget, Cuthbert, that it's not just you who's been doing all the soul-searching of late. I've had some confronting of my own to do. When you first told me you were – pardon me – heterosexual, I confess I was deeply troubled. Very deeply. I tried to hide it – badly, I'm sure – but I tried. And I tried to tell you the things you needed to hear, the things that would make you happy, because as your mother I am bound to do so. But that doesn't mean I haven't had to make adjustments (*Tapping her head.*) …in here. And regardless of my success or failure rate, I have at least been trying. (*Beat.*) Now, I seem to recall you explaining at great length how you'd struggled for so long to accept yourself as being heterosexual, and how you'd wrestled with your conscience and finally managed to fight your way to some sort of personal epiphany. And I listened, and I understood and I accepted what you said. But you seem to imagine that you can scoop up the entire maelstrom, dump it in my lap and expect me to react like Mary Poppins. Well, life's not like that, Cuthbert, and it's simply not fair. I need time to absorb it all, too. How much time I don't know. (*Beat.*) But apparently a month's not quite enough.

EILEEN

Age range: 40s – 60s

From the play *WYWH*, included in the collection *Going Solo: One-Act Plays for One Actor*.

Eileen, a good-humored but reclusive middle-aged divorcee has recently discovered a new life in the virtual world, thanks to some coaxing and encouragement from her nephew. Here she describes some of the joys and difficulties she experienced on her journey to creating her brand-new digital self.

I have presence...can you tell? Can't you feel it oozing out of my every pore? (*With a chuckle.*) No, probably not. That's because I don't – not in that sense, in the charismatic sense. Never did, really; not in all these years. Just ordinary, I suppose. Always have been. No one you'd notice...in particular. *But*, I do have *a* presence. A web presence, that is. There's another me floating around out there in the cosmos. It's a new and improved me that no one can see, they can only sense. It's another life and it's ever so much fun. (*Beat.*) My name's "Misti"...with an "I." That's to say, that's my alternative me's name, not the real me's name – my name. I wanted something with a bit of mystery to it, a bit of the unknown. And a touch of the poetic – a bit more poetic than "Eileen," at any rate. (*With a self-conscious laugh.*) And all right, yes, if I were being honest, maybe just a hint of the young and sexy, too. Well, why shouldn't I? It's a new me, I made it up – I can make it whatever I want it to be. Who's to know? No diets, no plastic surgeons, just re-label yourself and change a "Y" to an "I" and years of your life can just disappear in an instant. It's a modern-day miracle! (*Beat.*) Sam's the one who got me into all this. Sam's my nephew. He's a big whiz in the computer industry from what he tells me. Does all sorts of programming and coding and…whatever else it is they do. He's one of the best, from all accounts. Anyway, he's the one that pushed me online, as it were. He said I needed "modernizing," which I had a good laugh over. "Sam," I said, "I'm a woman of a certain age, not a 1970s prefab kitchen – there's not a lot you can do to change me at this stage in the game." "You'd be surprised," he said. And I was. Mind you, I will admit there were a few scenes and tantrums and one or two panic attacks along the way – not to mention the day I broke down in tears, sobbing that if I couldn't even set the toaster right to do dark brown instead of burned, how on earth was I going to communicate with 4 billion people across the globe, most of whom didn't speak English? But I got there…eventually. (*Looking down at her computer/tablet.*) I mastered this beast…this magic box.

SERIOCOMIC MONOLOGUES

Male

CUTHBERT

(Monologue 1)

Age range: 20s – 30s

From the play *Cuthbert's Last Stand.*

Playing matchmaker once more, Cuthbert's mother has brought home yet another young man as a potential suitor for her son. Having raised him in the hope that he is homosexual, her only dream was for him to live a full and interesting life beyond the insipid, middle-class customs and conventions that had stifled her own. Here, after being teased by his mother in front of their guest, Cuthbert's forbearance has finally reached its limit and he decides the time has come to confront his mother with the shocking truth that he knows can only break her heart.

That's right, go ahead and laugh. Laugh away. Get it *all* out of your system. Because when I've finished what I'm about to say, I doubt very much that laughter is going to be among your top ten list of immediate responses. (*With great difficulty.*) You see, I...I've no idea how many times I've attempted to tell you this in the past...and how many times my courage has simply up and left me, but I...I can't maintain this façade any longer, Mother. I can't continue with the lies...the deceit...the pretense. I can't go on saying one thing and feeling another. You see, the fact is, Mother, as hard as this is going to be for you to accept...or understand – especially when sober – the fact remains...the fact remains I am not the person you think I am. The painful truth is... (*Taking a deep breath.*) I am not...and as far as I know, never have been...a homosexual. (*Pause.*) Well? Aren't you going to say something? Aren't you going to tell me how...disappointed you are? How I've let you down? How ashamed you feel? (*Beat.*) I know this has to be difficult to take in, but I... I had to tell you. I couldn't continue living this make-believe existence any longer. (*Beat, then pensively.*) And now that I have told you, I...well, I feel...I feel wonderful, actually. And yet at the same time quite dreadful. Dreadful because...because I feel as though I've just taken the entire image of everything that you thought I was and smashed it into little tiny pieces.

VALENTINE

Age range: 20s – 30s (Cross-castable)

From the play *The End of the World*.

After years of shielding, nurturing, and home schooling their son, Valentine's parents decide that the time has finally arrived for him to make his own way in life. The bright but guileless Valentine is repelled by the prospect, but go he must, and here he recounts his first foray into the great big world that now beckons.

Cast out by my parents, the only people I'd ever truly known – the only love I'd ever experienced – I ventured forth into the vast world beyond. For miles I walked and wandered; mile upon mile upon mile of dank, drab, rainy streets, all of it with a heavy heart and an indescribable sense of trepidation. It seemed never ending – a soul-destroying maze of concrete and asphalt. In truth, I believe it could only have been a matter of 900 yards or so…but I was tired and disoriented. Everything seemed larger than life…exaggerated. Even the word 'exaggerated' seemed like an exaggeration somehow. (*Beat.*) My parents had sent me on my way with a small stipend and an enormous amount of love and goodwill. It didn't take me long to realise, however, that this was the reverse of what I actually needed. Their good intentions notwithstanding, a certain degree of resentment had begun to set in. Had I been fully prepared for this? For instance: common sense – a subject my father had given me countless lessons on, but the essence of which I was still at a loss to fully comprehend, since most of what he'd imparted related directly to his own particular life experience rather than some universal truth – did I have it? Could one even learn it? For the first time in my life I began to wonder if my parents were not, as I had always imagined them, the ultimate purveyors of the human experience. The very thought shook me to the core.

HORATIO

Age range: 20s – 50s (Cross-castable)

From the play *The Most Interesting Man in the Whole Wide World.*

Horatio Higgins loves nothing more than to impress the people he meets with fictitious, fanciful tales of his life and times – a result of his struggles with delusional disorder. Here he recalls the tragic and rather unusual circumstances under which his parents died.

As you may or may not recall, my mother and father were, to say the very, very least, very much in love. Madly, insanely so. Their love knew no bounds. Any descriptions or definitions of love that you may know of are meaningless compared to what they had. Their bond was inseparable – their passion indescribable. There is no literal definition of what they had – not in any language. It was immense, huge – beyond mere words. As the years went by, instead of becoming bored and restless with each other, their love and desire only intensified. There was no stopping it. It was something bigger than them, bigger than you or me – bigger than life itself. (*Beat.*) But, as with any great love story, tragedy loomed just around the corner. They'd gone to Montmartre for the weekend – their 30th anniversary. It was where they'd first met. Actually, it wasn't where they'd first met – they'd met at Croydon Technical College. But they'd both agreed it was where they wished they'd first met. And it was there, in that sweetly perfumed, badly lit and overpriced hotel room in Paris that they met their end. As they embraced each other for the final time, their bodies pressing up against one another in a frantic, wordless, insane collision of mindless love and abandonment they…quite horribly – and some might say inevitably – spontaneously combusted. (*Beat.*) Who can explain it? Who would dare? (*Beat.*) All that was left was ashes. Particles. Little tiny particles. Dust. And that is all we are. All of us. None of it's real. It's just forms. Different forms.

ART

Age range: 20s – 60s

From the play *The Curious Art of Critique*, included in the collection *The Meta Plays*.

It would appear, on the surface at least, that in The Curious Art of Critique, stage director Art is attempting to elicit stronger performances from two of his young actors in the production he's currently directing. Here Art, an effusive, mannered individual, is coaching Stephanie into delving deeper into the play so that she might give him more of what he's expecting from her.

Oh, Stephanie. Steph, Steph, Steph. Just look at you. Who could possibly find fault with you? (*Beat.*) Except me. (*Beat.*) You see, the problem is, Steph – and it's a big one – is that this play, despite its moments of levity, is in essence a work of *soul-destroying* tragedy. At its core, it is bleak, desolate, and utterly inconsolable. It has an ugly heart of darkness that is at once an indictment of the human condition and a testament to it. *That* is what I want it to show. *That* is what I want people to feel. Trust me, Steph, *believe* me, I can tell what a truly loving, feeling, caring person you are deep down inside…but all I'm seeing is an ice queen. You heard right. *But*…don't despair…well, do despair, that's the point…*but*, I think I may have a solution for you. I'm sure you're very familiar with the teachings of Constantin Stanislavski and of his system, and most especially of his introduction of the use of emotion memory. And *that* is what I want from you, Steph. I want you to *feel* the raw pain of what's happening on stage by internally reliving some unspeakable, painful, catastrophic event that occurred in your own life. So, come on – what do you have? Dig deep, Stephanie. I want real human misery. So what is it? There has to be something. Something that scarred you like nothing else. Something that shut your world down. Something that still tortures you to this very day. The love of your life that dumped you for your best friend? A dearly beloved pet that passed away? A relative gassed in the Holocaust? Anything, something – you have to give me s*omething*, Stephanie.

CUTHBERT

(Monologue 2)

Age range: 20s – 30s

From the play *Cuthbert's Last Stand.*

Contrary to all her hopes and expectations, Mrs. Pennington-South's son, Cuthbert, is not homosexual – a fact she's just been forced to confront by her son's open admittance of his heterosexuality. Unfortunately, her initial reaction to this revelation doesn't go well, and here Cuthbert attempts to help his mother understand the dilemma her ambitions had placed him in.

It's worth keeping in mind that despite the coming out scenario being turned on its head to comic effect here, the depth of feeling and passion that Cuthbert is experiencing in this moment is very real and heartfelt.

My God, Mother, if you *only knew!* If you only knew the amount of times that I'd tried to convince myself that I was a homosexual – because I wanted to make you happy…because I wanted to make you proud of me. I'd repeat it and repeat it and repeat it in my mind until the words lost all their meaning. But none of it made a jot of difference. I may as well have been trying to convince myself that I was…Bishop Desmond Tutu…because…because somehow that truth that I didn't want to face – that I had tried so hard to submerge – would always rise back up to the top. It was like curdled milk in a cup of tea: it didn't matter how many times I'd stir it around and around because sooner or later there it was again, floating about on the surface in dizzying circles. I couldn't make go away. (*Beat.*) I began to feel haunted. It was like having a guillotine hovering tenuously above my neck. I felt that if the truth were ever known it would come plunging down and tear through everything that had constituted my life. (*Beat.*) And then one day...one day I just stopped fighting it. One day I realised that I couldn't continue to live my life simply in order to please you...or father, or young Tristram here, or anyone else for that matter. I knew I had to stop pretending and hiding and...and start living my life for me – because it's mine. And that day, Mother...that day...was today.

CHARACTER

Age range: 20s – 60s (Cross-castable)

From the play *A Flawed Character*, included in the collection *The Meta Plays*.

The flawed character in the abovementioned play is indeed just that – a character in a play that the playwright who created him now finds to be an imperfect creation that's hampering his progress on the script. Infuriated by the writer's apparent inability or reluctance to flesh him out, the character turns on his creator and lets him know just exactly what he thinks of him.

Now you just listen to me. I have sat here patiently while you've made every effort to do anything and everything except follow through on what you started. I've stared into space, I've yawned, I've twiddled my thumbs, I've even – in my excruciating boredom – tried very hard to imagine a life for myself out of my own head. But I can't. Only you have the power to do that, you supercilious, self-important, self-pitying, self-indulgent, self-aggrandizing...self! You think you're so high and mighty, but let me tell you something – one day...one day, when you're lying on some cold, hard park bench, stinking of urine and coughing up snot, I'll be there. I'll be there, and I'll be laughing; laughing so hard. Laughing and clapping and dancing and singing and celebrating everything that makes you utterly disgusting yet still cling to life because you don't have the guts to kill yourself. (*Beat.*) See, I think it's high time you took a long, hard look in the mirror, buddy. Then you'll come face-to-face with the real non-starter around here. You prance around this place like some pretentious dick-on-a-stick, thinking you're so artistic, and so literary. "Look at me, I'm a writer." "Look at me, I'm a playwright; I'm so intellectual; I'm so esoteric; a struggling, penniless martyr to my art." "I go forth like Quixote, noble and proud in the face of the doubters and non-believers, and do it all with my head held high and a fountain pen rammed up my precious, tortured ass!"(*Beat.*) But what do you really do, *really?* Not much of anything, really. You just like to *think* you do, because it makes you feel important. It makes you feel like you *matter.* But guess what? News flash – *ya don't!* Hate to break it to ya, buddy – but ya ain't curin' cancer here.

MALCOLM

Age range: 20s – 50s

From the play *A Small Act of Vandalism*, included in the collection *Going Solo: One-Act Plays for One Actor*.

It's the small act of vandalism of the title that Malcolm discusses here, as he relays the sequence of events that led to him defiling a very expensive piece of china. The title also refers to a far sadder and more consequential act in Malcolm's tale, but here the warmhearted but troubled man recounts one of the more lighthearted moments from his story.

I keep Mother's ashes in a little Wedgwood box. Very expensive, it was. Very expensive indeed. But worth it – worth every penny – 'cause Mother was worth it. But now I keep it glued shut, actually. The lid, that is. I glued it myself with superglue – I had to. Seems criminal, really, doing something like that to a beautiful piece of genuine Wedgwood bone china. But it had to be done. I had no choice. Not after the, um…well…the incident. (*Beat.*) The thing is, I loved Mother, you see, and I missed her something terrible. Anyway…some days…evenings…when I missed her most, I'd sit down and have a chat with her. Just me and her and a bottle of pale ale…having a chitchat. I'd sit her down on the coffee table, take the lid off, open up a pale ale, light up a cigarette, and tell her all that was on my mind – just like before…before she…took her leave. (*Beat.*) But then, one evening…oh, about two or three months ago now, I suppose…I had…let's just say, one of my *off days*. At first I tried to hide it from her. I just chatted about this and that –

general things, you know – and I'd pour another pale ale, and have another cigarette…and another pale ale, and another cigarette…and another, and another…and I suppose it all started to get a bit carried away, and all these feelings started bubbling up out of nowhere, and just as I was telling her how angry I was with her, I saw myself flick the ash from my cigarette into her little Wedgwood resting place instead of the ashtray! (*Beat.*) I froze. (*Beat.*) I was horrified. Mortified. How could I have done such a thing? To my own Mother? It was the ultimate slap in the face. And what could I do? I couldn't fish it out – it all looked the same. I could've scooped out the top part, I suppose…but some of that was Mother. Anyway, eventually I apologized to her very sincerely and without a scene, and vowed that the next morning I would seal the lid of her little Wedgwood tomb permanently and for all eternity – just like the ancient Pharaohs and Cleopatra, etcetera. (*Beat.*) So yes, even though in most respects that is my Mother, I suppose that, strictly speaking, I'd have to say that it's 99.8% my Mother…and a tiny little bit of Marlboro Light.

"Acting is all about honesty. If you can fake that, you've got it made."

~ George Burns

ABOUT THE AUTHOR

From the Royal Court Theatre in London to the Playhouse Theatre in Tasmania, the works of playwright Andrew Biss have been performed across the globe, spanning four continents. His plays have won awards on both coasts of the U.S., critical acclaim in the U.K., and quickly became an Off-Off-Broadway mainstay.

In London his plays have been performed at The Royal Court Theatre, Theatre503, Riverside Studios, The Union Theatre, The White Bear Theatre, The Brockley Jack Studio Theatre, Fractured Lines Theatre & Film at COG ARTSpace, and Ghost Dog Productions at The Horse & Stables.

In New York his plays have been produced at Theatre Row Studios, The Samuel French Off-Off-Broadway Festival, The Kraine Theater, The Red Room Theater, Times Square Arts Center, Manhattan Theatre Source, Mind The Gap Theatre, 3Graces Theatre Company, Curan Repertory Company, Emerging Artists Theatre, Pulse Ensemble Theatre, American Globe Theatre, The American Theater of Actors, and Chashama Theatres, among others.

His plays and monologues are published in numerous anthologies from trade publishers Bedford/St. Martin's, Smith & Kraus, Inc., Pioneer Drama Service, and Applause Theatre & Cinema Books.

A former actor, Andrew appeared in a multitude of stage

productions from London to Los Angeles, along with various film and television appearances, most notably in director Francis Ford Coppola's Bram Stoker's Dracula.

Originally from England, Andrew is a long-time resident of the United States. He is a graduate of the University of the Arts London, and a member of the Dramatists Guild of America, Inc.

For more information please visit his website at:

www.andrewbiss.com

Made in the USA
Las Vegas, NV
27 November 2022